TALES

from the

ENDS *of the* EARTH

TALES
from the
ENDS *of the* EARTH

My Adventures in East Africa and Beyond

TODD GUSTAFSON

TALES *from the* ENDS *of the* EARTH
My Adventures in East Africa and Beyond

First Edition
Copyright © 2025 by Todd Gustafson

Published by
To the Ends of the Earth, LLC

For permission requests, contact MunnAvenuePress.com

Paperback ISBN: 978-1-969679-15-5
Hardcover ISBN: 978-1-969679-16-2
Printed in the United States of America

For my friend Jane Goodall

"What you do makes a difference, and you have to decide what kind of a difference you want to make."

Dr. Jane Goodall, UN Messenger of Peace
1934-2025

TABLE OF CONTENTS

PREFACE

Before you get started, you need to know that I have had an extraordinary life, and the people in my world have possessed world-class talents. My mom had the voice of an angel. Dad was a teacher of biology and zoology. He had an engaging, operatic tenor voice that stood him in good stead in the early days of television. He sang at Carnegie Hall with the Great One, Swedish tenor Jussi Björling. In another career, he ran a one-man machine shop, making specialty parts for NASA, Bendix Aviation, and Sundstrand Aerospace. He was there at Julius Nyerere's inauguration when he was made the first president of the brand-new republic of Tanzania.

My brother Brian lived with Hadzabe bushmen, tracked lions with George Adamson, a central character in Joy Adamson's *Born Free* book and movie, and tossed back a whiskey or two with Bill Woodley, founder of Kenya's Tsavo National Park.

My wife Julie is at the top of her field in business and has the amazing superpower of being organized. Her love, support, and planning skills are the reasons I am able to accomplish any of my goals at the ends of the earth.

I am both a professional musician and wildlife photographer. I've played trumpet for European royalty and performed at the jazz festivals at Montreux, North Sea, Nice, and Paris. I toured with the Temptations and *Tonight Show* drummer Ed Shaughnessy, among others, and recorded jazz CDs with top studio musicians in the world.

My nature photos have won awards in the BBC Wildlife Photographer of the Year and *Nature's Best* competitions, have been published in *Time,* and have graced covers of *Scientific American, Nature's Best,* and Nikon's full product guides.

I've also photographed Tina Turner, Wynton Marsalis, Robert Downey Jr., Al Pacino, the band Chicago, and many others on my artistic journey.

This book contains stories that chronicle what it took to make dramatic, award-winning photographs and television documentaries at the ends of the earth.

PART ONE

The Evolution of a Concept

To the Ends of the Earth Books

These safari stories are the foundation upon which *To the Ends of the Earth* was built. Our early prints, taken during those first expeditions, were displayed throughout our home as daily reminders of the wild places we had experienced. With each journey, the photography evolved, becoming more refined and powerful. One day, Julie suggested that we find a way to share these images with a broader audience, using the proceeds to support meaningful conservation efforts.

What began as a simple concept—a portfolio of twenty-four curated prints—quickly grew into a more ambitious vision: a set of three 20 x 20-inch fine art books. I transformed our basement into a full-scale print studio, installing two industrial-grade printers. I sourced custom 20-by-40-inch double-sided paper from a supplier in Hollywood to match my design specifications. Each page was meticulously planned: most featured a single image, some spanned two pages, and four special pages unfolded into dramatic 80-inch panoramic spreads.

Despite the chorus of voices insisting, "It can't be done," we proved

Book collector John Dupps receiving his Museum Edition of the
To the Ends of the Earth three-volume set

otherwise. The final product—*To the Ends of the Earth: East Africa, Birds of East Africa*, and *The Natural World*—earned widespread acclaim. Book and art collectors have described the set as the most lavish since Audubon's legendary 1800s folios, and each volume includes a foreword penned by conservation giants Jane Goodall, Peter Raven, and Carl Safina.

TO THE ENDS OF THE EARTH DOCUMENTARIES

A producer at PBS in St. Louis happened upon the book collection and posed a surprising question: Had I ever considered making a documentary about how the books were created? My initial thought? *That sounds like a snooze-fest. You shoot the photos, print the pages, bind the books, and you ship them*—hardly riveting cinema.

But he pushed back immediately: "No, no, no. We want to see how a professional photographer actually gets out there, into the wild, and captures the kinds of images that stir people to care about the natural world." That, I realized, was a story worth telling.

Fortunately, I had some decent video footage from an earlier East Africa project, and though my video-editing skills were basic at best, I stitched together a demo reel that included a striking clip of flamingos on the move. When it was ready, I invited Michael and Dawn—veterans of the Broadway production world, to give it a look. They watched politely and offered kind words. But then, at the end, Michael said, "Hold on. Rewind that."

He stopped the video at the moment when hyenas exploded into a sea of flamingos. The footage cut to me explaining what we were witnessing.

"That guy," Michael said, pointing at the screen. "I want more of that guy. Tell us what we're seeing. Why it matters. What did it take to get that shot?" Dawn nodded in agreement, and just like that, we had the blueprint for the *To the Ends of the Earth* documentary series.

Since then, we've produced five films:

- *East Africa*
- *Birds of East Africa*
- *The Natural World*
- *Oceans*
- *Avian Chronicles*

The series now airs on PBS in 94% of U.S. television markets and broadcasts in thirty-six countries worldwide.

COMPOSING A FILM SCORE

My next creative hurdle was music, and it was a steep one. Without it, the documentary risked being more of a cinematic lullaby than a compelling experience. The task? Compose a full film score. The challenge? I had a track record of failure in music theory and enough piano trauma to last a lifetime. And yet, I had one major advantage: years spent in recording booths around the world. I knew what I wanted it to *sound* like.

So, I sat at the piano and began playing the music I heard in my head. I started with the Main Theme—something bold, unforgettable. It took me

Jo Ann Daugherty editing the documentary film score

an entire afternoon to shape the piece. That night, while watching *Game of Thrones*, a familiar-sounding melody crept into a scene featuring a lone rider. Julie's eyes widened. "Wait—isn't that your theme?"

Cue me, sinking into the couch and tossing my carefully crafted, handwritten score in the trash.

Determined, I returned to the piano the next day and wrote a new theme, richer this time, with suspensions, key changes, and anything else I could dredge up from my less-than-stellar understanding of music composition.

I brought the piece to Jo Ann, a Broadway powerhouse and virtuoso pianist. As she played, I recorded. Her interpretation transformed my scribbled draft into something alive, with countermelodies and narrative depth. Her husband Ryan joined in, adding percussion, and suddenly, we had a sound that could inspire emotion.

I dove into editing the moment I got home. But it quickly became clear. Four minutes of piano music wouldn't cut it for a one-hour documentary. I needed more music. A lot more.

So, the next day, I got back to composing. It's worth noting my musical résumé includes bombing piano class so badly in college that I purposefully broke my pinkie to escape a proficiency test (yes, really). In hindsight, practicing might've been a better option. But here I was, decades later, hunting for melodies that matched the spirit of the film. And somehow, despite the scars, the music kept coming. I can't help but wonder if my college music theory teacher would have a heart attack if he got wind of me attempting to compose actual music.

Back to composing the score—this time with clarity and instinct guiding my hands. As I sat at the piano, I realized the melodies were already there, waiting. I could hear the pulse of the savannah, the grace of elephants, the playful energy of leopard cubs, and the thunderous rhythm of the great migration. I began to shape those impressions note by note, carefully transcribing each melody and harmony onto music paper.

Every time I finished a batch of three compositions, I brought them to Jo Ann, whose keen musical ear and artistry brought polish and power to each piece. Over about two months, this process resulted in 22 original compositions. Each one was a musical reflection of the natural world that had inspired it. The soundtrack began to breathe with its own life.

It didn't take long to realize that solo piano, no matter how expressive, wouldn't hold a viewer's interest for a full hour of film viewing. I needed more sonic depth. I needed something bold and textured. During a chat with Chicago Symphony Orchestra trumpeter John Hagstrom (yes, that John Hagstrom. I did mention I know some top-tier talent), he suggested, "Why not reach out to Gary Fry? He orchestrates the CSO's major events and holiday programs."

The idea hadn't crossed my mind, but it clicked instantly. I'd once photographed Gary receiving a lifetime achievement award and hoped that connection might open the door. So, I called him, described the scope of the project, and without hesitation—literally within three seconds—he replied, "I'd love to be involved. Let's meet this week to go over the details."

*Todd and Gary Fry at
Ocean Way Studio*

The Nashville Music Scoring Orchestra

We sat down soon after, and Gary immediately grasped what the score needed. "Here's the plan," he said. "We'll record in Nashville at Ocean Way Studio with the sixty-five-piece Nashville Music Scoring Orchestra. Then we'll mix the tracks in Chicago, and it'll all be wrapped in two weeks."

With the final orchestrated recording in hand, I dove into editing, and the film finally began to take on its full, cinematic shape.

Now, the only piece missing was the narrator.

JANE GOODALL

I wasn't comfortable with the thought of me doing all the narration for the film. I needed it to be someone with gravitas and a recognizable voice. We made lists of names of people we thought would fit the bill. Morgan Freeman, John Goodman, Joe Buck, John Hamm, and Ian McShane were all on that list. While each would work, we started looking in a new direction, one that included giants in the conservation world. We contacted Sir David Attenborough, Peter Raven, and Carl Safina. Some were interested but not available, and some were available, but not exposed to the project enough to be interested.

My number one choice had always been Jane Goodall, but she is constantly on the road and has a serious stable of "gatekeepers" that monitor her correspondence. She had written the forward to the East Africa book, so I thought we had a chance. I had sent her an inquiry a year before and hadn't received a reply, when out of the blue, there in my email inbox, was a message from Jane herself. She would be in Chicago on a specific date. But it was a date on which I would be in Tanzania. She sent another date when she would be in Tanzania . . . and I would be in Chicago. It went on like this for a month. I had almost given up hope when, while filming jaguars on a trip to Brazil, I got another message. Jane would be in Seattle in two days. I would be finishing the jaguar trip and flying home in two days.

I replied with a resounding, "Yes! I will meet you in Seattle."

It's a Go!

I had Julie book a flight to Seattle and reserve a hotel room at the Fairmont Hotel, where Jane was staying. It cost $1,600 a night. That was a little bit steep for my budget, so Julie got a room down the street for $100. I contacted a friend at Dr. Caw Recording Studio, who agreed to lend me some top-of-the-line German microphones for recording Jane's voice-over. When I landed at O'Hare International, Julie had everything packed up. She met me at the check-in counter, gave me the case, and I got on the flight to Seattle.

When I landed, I called Jane's handlers to confirm the following day's script reading. They said it would be fine for them to come to my room at noon. I told them I was in a different hotel, which prompted them to say the recording would be canceled. It was devastating!

But after a few minutes, I was able to come up with a plan. I hightailed it to the Fairmont Hotel and asked for the concierge. He was out for the next few days, but someone from the front desk could help me. "Someone from the front desk" turned out to be the kindest, most helpful young woman I could ever have hoped for.

"How can I help?"

I explained that I did not have a reservation at the Fairmont, but that I was scheduled for a noon interview tomorrow. "Is there a room I could use for the script reading?" I asked.

She answered, "Of course. Let's see what we have available."

She showed me several venues that wouldn't work for one reason or another, till she showed me "The Camelot Room." It was perfect. It had eighteen-foot walnut walls covered with tapestries, lush carpeting, and a twelve-foot cherrywood table. She said I could set up an hour early and have it for the rest of the day. I called Jane's people and confirmed the time and place.

The Recording

At noon the following day, I had the mics and lighting set up and the script printed. My original thought had been to have Jane read three paragraphs from her book forward, but on the plane from Brazil, I extracted and wrote sixteen pages of script that I would be able to use in the documentary. The front desk trainee had made large print copies that would be perfect for Jane to read.

I waited in the hall for Jane to arrive and got a case of the jitters when her entourage started walking down the hall toward me. I reached out for her

Todd with Jane Goodall, reviewing the Museum Edition of the
East Africa book

hand and said, "I've been waiting my whole life for this. Hello, Jane Goodall!"

With a reserved smile, she answered, "I knew who your father was." We entered the room, got comfortable with the setup, and adjusted mics and lighting.

She looked through the script as her handler peppered me with questions: "Where will this be used? Who will see it? How long is the script? That's simply too long and not fair to others who work with Dr. Goodall!"

"That will be quite all right," Jane broke in. "It's a fine script and his books are lovely." *Whew*!

As I started recording, Jane chimed in, "Are we rolling—with sound?" She proceeded to read the entire 16-page script in one take!

When she read the last line, she stated, "I must be off. I have a radio interview in five minutes."

I responded, "I wish we had more time. I have some book pages I would love for you to sign, and I brought the Museum Edition of *To the Ends of the Earth: East Africa* book for you as a thank you gift for your generous voice-over."

"It's quite all right," she said. "I'll be back in 45 minutes."

As the door closed, I couldn't help but think how lucky I was with the way things were turning out. At that moment, the door burst open and Jane trundled toward me, arms open wide. "What—no hug?"

Just as she left the second time, I got a text from Julie with a photo of the newest *National Geographic* magazine with the headline "Being Jane" with a photo of an impossibly young Jane Goodall arriving at Gombe Reserve in 1960. I ran to the bookstore down the block and bought ten copies that Jane signed on her return from the radio interview. She also invited me to attend her presentation that night.

A Night to Remember

As powerful and intriguing as her presentation was, what followed was one of the highlights of my life. As the presentation wound down, Jane invited the guests to pick up her newest book from a stack of pre-signed copies. As she walked by the tower of books, she whispered, "Don't make it obvious, but follow me."

I looked around and saw her handlers near the room's double doors. As they escorted Jane out of the room, I followed. The doors were closing. Jane grabbed my arm, saying, "Now, run!"

What followed was a mad dash to the elevator bank at the end of the hall. As the doors were closing, I could see the guests from the book-signing spilling into the hallway and charging toward us. It looked like a scene from a zombie apocalypse movie!

"They never want an event to end," Jane whispered as we exited the elevator on the penthouse floor. We entered the suite and Jane reached for a gold leaf box with a distinctive silver logo on it—Chivas Regal scotch whiskey.

Looking at me, she said, "Fetch me some crystal tumblers, will you, please. It's that kind of night!"

We stayed up till 3:00 a.m., talking about old days, mutual friends, the future of the planet, and more.

PART TWO

Safari Tales

A LEOPARD FAMILY

I've followed a Serengeti leopard family for generations. One August, we discovered the mother with two-month-old cubs emerging from the rocky outcrops. They played and nursed for hours, completely at ease in their hidden sanctuary.

The following season, we found them again, this time in a breathtaking scene. All three perched together on the branch of a towering fig tree, the vast Serengeti stretching endlessly behind them.

By the third season, we searched the familiar rock formations that had been their home, combing through the kopjes with no sign of them. After an hour of searching, we prepared to leave, winding out of the rocky terrain toward camp. A safari vehicle appeared seemingly out of nowhere, pulling up beside us. The driver, a female guide, rare in the safari world, was strikingly beautiful. She spoke with quiet confidence.

"Follow me, and I will give you leopards," she said before turning and driving away.

I turned to Salvatory. "We have to follow her. She's Malaika!" which is

Swahili for "angel."

He hesitated. "No. She doesn't know where they are." But despite his doubts, he followed.

A half hour passed. I questioned whether she truly knew the leopards' whereabouts. "Of course she does," Salva said, now certain. "She's Malaika."

Another half hour of winding tracks brought us to a narrow dirt track. My doubts resurfaced. "I think she's lost. We may never make it back!"

Then, just over a ridge, across a golden grass-covered valley, her vehicle stopped. She pointed ahead, and, as if summoned by fate, two spotted heads lifted from the tall grass. It was them, the leopard brother and sister we'd been searching for. They'd reached the age where their mother had left them to fend for themselves. But more than that, they had matured to the point where they were about to part ways forever.

I had heard stories of this moment, a final farewell between leopard siblings, but had never seen it myself or knew of anyone who had. We eased into position as the two leopards circled each other. Then suddenly, they leapt straight up, spinning in midair in a synchronized, effortless display. It was a ballet of epic proportions, graceful, fierce, mesmerizing. They danced, chased, and twirled around the meadow, an elegant final performance, until at last, they paused. Then, without a sound, they turned and walked away from each other, disappearing into the wilderness.

My heart pounded in my chest. Had we truly just witnessed this once-in-a-lifetime moment? I wanted to thank Malaika, to express my gratitude for leading us to this extraordinary event. But when we searched for her vehicle, it was gone. Nothing but open savannah stretched out before us. Had she ever truly been there, or had she been something else entirely, an angel who vanished after fulfilling her purpose?

The next day, we found the brother sunning himself on a boulder, four kilometers from the meadow. The sister was hunting in the valley, three kilometers away in the opposite direction.

Leopards' farewell dance

RHINOS AND A SERVAL CAT

Let's begin with a bit of natural history. Rhinoceroses are among the most ancient and largest living land animals. White rhinos are the most abundant of the five remaining species, and have broad, flat lips; their name is surmised to be from misinterpreting the Afrikaans word for "wide." The black rhino, called black not for its color but to distinguish it from the white, is the most common species in Tanzania. Black rhinos are identified by their prehensile lips, ideal for foraging, and their smaller size. They are still formidable, with weights up to 3,000 pounds. Rhinos are the second-largest land mammal after elephants. Black rhinos are critically endangered due to poaching and habitat loss.

One place to observe black rhinos is in the Ngorongoro Crater, but the population is small and sightings are infrequent. There are vast plains within the Crater where they can wander undisturbed and are often far from roads making them hard to find. Strict rules govern viewing distances and the

A serval cat pounces on its prey.

position of vehicles to ensure that rhinos have a clear escape route. The park stringently prohibits blocking the path of a rhino.

Photographing these impressive animals presents other challenges as well, the first being that everyone wants to photograph a rhino! They are the most inaccessible of the Big Five. If a rhino does approach a road, drivers broadcast the news, and other vehicles arrive in anticipation of its crossing. In addition, black rhinos can be unpredictable, either foraging in a slow, meandering fashion and turning back, or suddenly charging between the cars at impressive speeds.

In contrast, serval cats are the exotic jewels of Africa's plains. These graceful felines are two to three times the size of a house cat and are built for stealth and agility, with long legs, a slender neck, striking spots, and notably large ears. Efficient hunters, their oversized ears allow them to hear subtle rustlings of mice and voles. Their powerful legs can launch them into astonishing leaps, and their gold-and-black patterned fur provides perfect camouflage. After eight years on safari, I had never seen one of these beautiful, elusive creatures.

We were in the heart of the Crater when the call came through: a rhino was heading toward the road near the Munge River. The report indicated it was moving slowly, giving us hope that we would arrive in time. Our driver flew over the dirt roads to get there, but as we neared the site, we could see that we were too late. The massive animal had already sprinted across the road and was vanishing into the plains.

Dismayed at missing the shot, we aimlessly wandered the Munge area until a crackle on the radio brought more exciting news. We heard a driver announce, "Another rhino is approaching the road near the Lerai Forest.

Hurry!"

We immediately sped to the opposite side of the Crater. I couldn't believe we had a second chance to photograph rhinos! When we flew past a stretch where the road dipped between surrounding grasslands, Julie whispered something under her breath.

"What?" I asked, as we bumped along.

"Serval cat," she mumbled. Her voice was barely audible.

"What?"

"Serval cat. There was a serval cat."

By the time her words registered, we were already a half-mile past the sighting. Quickly, we doubled back to locate the spot where she had seen the elusive feline. There it was, walking away, now nearly 200 yards distant.

"Why didn't you just yell 'Serval cat'?" I asked.

"I didn't want to interrupt while you were so focused on reaching the rhino," she said.

I blinked, shook my head, and then broke out laughing. Soon we both couldn't stop. It was true. I had rhino fever. "Then let's get to the rhino!"

By the time we arrived, it was again too late. That rhino was a mile away, heading toward the Crater's far side.

One thing I have learned about safaris is that what you miss the first time might be just around the next bend. The next morning, Julie spotted two rhinos heading right toward us. We had enough time to position our vehicle and take great images of these magnificent animals.

Black rhinos in Ngorongoro Crater

And from that day on, no member of our family can see a serval cat without whispering at half volume, "Serval cat!"

DISASTER IN THE MOZAMBIQUE CHANNEL

It was October in Madagascar, the season of courtship for crab plovers. These subtly beautiful shorebirds patrol the mudflats of the Indian Ocean, searching for ghost crabs. During mating season, males catch a crab, present it to a female, and carefully place it on her beak. With a flick of her head, she tosses the crab into the air, catches, and devours it. Mating follows. I had witnessed and photographed this ritual on Kenya's coast, but I had never filmed it. This trip to Madagascar was carefully planned to put us in the right place at the right time to capture the event.

Seven of us embarked on this adventure, a crew seemingly straight out of a television cast. I played Gilligan, the Aussie was the Skipper, the oncologist played the Professor, the entomologist was Ginger, her sister became Mary Ann, and the remaining two sisters took on the roles of Thurston Howell and Lovey. We set off into the Betsiboka Delta for a three-hour tour.

Crab plover courtship

The Betsiboka is a massive, dynamic delta, so vast and vibrant that it's visible from space. Its intense red hue comes from soil erosion and the runoff caused by the slash-and-burn farming practices pervasive in Madagascar. Our mission was to navigate the labyrinthine channels and track down the elusive crab plovers. As we explored, we encountered a variety of fascinating wading birds and vibrant kingfishers, but no sign of the plovers. We theorized that their feeding and courtship rituals must be tied to the tides. A particularly promising mudflat was slowly emerging as the tide receded, and we hoped the plovers would soon arrive.

Under the relentless tropical sun, we stayed hydrated while waiting. Thirty minutes passed, but still no plovers. We decided to move on, but there was just one problem: we couldn't. Not only had we run aground, but the captain had been napping, neglecting the tides, and one of our two motors wasn't working. We were stuck, at least until the tide shifted, which wouldn't happen for another six hours.

The Aussie turned to me with grim certainty. "We're fu@ked," he declared.

"Yes," I agreed. "We're low on water and have no shade."

But the Aussie, who was well-acquainted with the perils of coastal waters, had even bigger concerns.

"Nope," he said. "I checked the mouth of the delta yesterday at this time. When the tide turns, the waves will be eight-footers. We're not making it back alive in this boat."

I attempted optimism. "I'm sure it'll be fine."

Six hours later, the tide finally returned, lifting our barely functional craft off the mudflat. The captain fired up the single working engine and sped out of the channel with the Aussie and me up front, two sets of sisters, the oncologist, and our guide in the back, and the captain at the helm.

The Aussie had not been exaggerating. As soon as we rounded the headland, monstrous waves slammed into the boat, tossing us up, down, and side-to-side. After an hour of this battering, I could see the tiny beach where we were supposed to land. There was no dock, just sand. The plan was simple enough: drop anchor far enough offshore and allow the boat to drift in for a safe landing, then disembark and walk to our hotel. That would not

Shipwreck in the Mozambique Channel

be happening. Our boat floundered in the troughs of towering waves, facing away from the beach.

The Aussie and I were tightly clutching our cameras to keep them from spilling overboard. The boat lurched to starboard, tossing the Aussie into me. Then a roll to port threw me across the deck, landing directly on top of him. I had no idea what was happening behind us until I glanced back and saw the anchor sitting idly on the back deck. There was no captain. He had been washed overboard. We were at the mercy of the waves.

As the boat tumbled toward shore, I caught sight of a dozen children playing in the surf, directly in our path. They didn't seem alarmed, merely curious, as if wondering how this would all unfold. Suddenly, I heard our guide shouting in panic, "Get out of the boat! Now!" His eyes were wide with urgency.

I had my camera gear in hand and prepared to jump, but hesitation struck me. As I balanced on the gunwale, I glanced at my new hiking boots. *Huh*, I thought. *I really don't want to get these wet. Maybe I could wait a little longer.*

Just then, the boat lurched violently, launching me into the shallow surf. I was safe. My boots were soaked. But my camera gear had survived. The others had already scrambled onto the shore and were staring at our beached vessel, wondering where the captain had gone. A hundred yards down the beach, he emerged, head hanging low, aware that his carelessness could have turned this near-disaster into a true tragedy.

We all stood there looking bedraggled but miraculously unhurt. On our walk back to the hotel, we debated whether this disaster had been more like "The Wreck of the *Edmond Fitzgerald*," *The Poseidon Adventure*, or the fateful tale of the *SS Minnow*.

JACKSON'S WIDOWBIRDS

One of my favorite roads in Tanzania's Ngorongoro Crater angles through the territory of the Munge lion pride. I have often photographed cubs playing in the fields on either side of this track, and my driver always goes slowly so we can look carefully.

This time, there were no lions, but I saw a quick movement out of the corner of my eye. Something was popping up and down in the grass. And not just one something, but dozens! Jackson's widowbirds! I had seen a drawing

of one in a book in 1986 and never thought I'd ever encounter one in the wild. Breeding males are mostly black, with rufous wings and long, luxurious tails. But as beautiful as they are, it is their breeding display that makes them exceptional. Females are attracted to both the tail feathers and the quality of a male's display.

In breeding season, dozens of male widowbirds gather at a lek and display for females. The word "lek" derives from the Swedish word for "play or dance." In the

Male widowbird mating display

case of Jackson's widowbirds, the dance move is to jump high off the ground, float and stabilize in the air, then land in the same spot, all the while flashing their tail feathers. After twenty or more leaps, all the males fly to perches. They sing and wave their gorgeous tails until there is a signal to restart the hopping dance.

Photographing these birds was like playing the Whac-A-Mole arcade game, where moles rapidly jump out of holes at random intervals. My camera and I were now in a new game of Whack-A-Widowbird—not to be confused with my toddler son's pronunciation of "little bird." Even with the camera set at twenty frames per second, it was easy to completely miss the bird, so easy that my first 500 shots were entirely of grass.

I told myself not to panic, but that was the first thing I did. Was I going to miss every shot? *Don't panic, don't panic,* I kept telling myself, while fumbling with teleconverters and switching lenses. I figured out the timing of their jumps and focused only on birds in the best light, jumping at an appropriate distance with bodies angled sideways to the camera.

My next goal was to film the behavior without the camera refocusing on the grass when the birds landed. Stills were a challenge, but video seemed impossible. That night, I looked through the camera's instruction manual and found a technique that I thought would work.

We went out the next day, desperately hoping the birds would still be displaying. After an interminable drive through the Crater and up the sidetrack, we reached the lek. The widowbirds were still leaping and flaunting their feathers. Now for the new focusing technique. When I found a bird in the right spot and jumping at the correct angle, I focused on it in midair and hit a button that disabled the autofocus. It worked! Every time a bird jumped and landed in the same place, the next jumps were all in focus, sometimes as many as twenty-five in a row.

Sweet victory! It was an engaging species, doing a dramatic behavior in a perfect setting, in great light. And the photos were executed flawlessly with professional equipment!

THREE LEOPARDS IN A TREE

Leopards are magnificent, territorial, secretive cats—always an exciting subject for a photo shoot. During my time in Tanzania, I've come to know the local leopard population well. Although it is popular to assign names to wild animals, names like Cassy, Kwitonda, or research terms like S-32 strip away an animal's untamed essence and cheapen the thrill of discovery for me.

We've followed and become familiar with some Serengeti leopard families through five generations. Respecting their wild and free existence, we've identified them simply as the Mother, the Daughter, or, when a formidable new adversary arrived in the territory, the Stranger.

One early morning, while navigating a winding track, we found ourselves in the territory of the Daughter, who was raising two-year-old cubs. In the past, we had watched her play, train, and hunt with them, and I fervently hoped to catch another glimpse of them on this trip.

I jokingly asked Julie, "Can you please find a leopard?"

She laughed. "The only way I'd ever spot one is if she were walking down the road straight at us."

And in an astonishing twist, the moment we rounded the next curve,

A leopard family relaxes on a single branch

three leopards were on the road directly in front of us! Julie pointed and said, with a twinkle in her eye, "Leopards." They walked toward us, and we slowly reversed for half a mile, watching them vanish into the tall grass.   We remained in the area, patiently waiting and occasionally spying ears or tails as the cubs climbed into low bushes and small trees. Watching their antics was exhilarating, though not ideal for photography. A few minutes later, we noticed a flicker of movement. It was a leopard's tail gliding through the tall grass and heading to a towering fig tree in the distance. Thinking this could be their home base, we hurried to position ourselves near the tree. We arrived just in time to find the mother already settled on a picturesque branch, with her cubs springing up to greet her.

What followed was pure photographic bliss. We had an hour of uninterrupted magic as the three leopards groomed, stretched, and relaxed on the same branch, framed perfectly against the vast Serengeti backdrop. The images captured that day remain some of the most cherished and successful shots of my career.

LION PRIDES

Lions possess one of the most intricate social structures in the animal kingdom. A pride typically consists of dominant males, adult females, sub-adults, and cubs—each with a distinct role in the survival and success of the group. Cubs are the future of the pride and are fiercely protected. Sub-adults hone their survival skills through playful interactions with each other, the cubs, and adults. Adult females are the primary hunters, responsible for feeding the pride and nursing the young. They often travel long distances in search of prey. Males safeguard the pride's territory and ensure their lineage continues. Though they may sleep up to 22 hours a day, they remain acutely aware of everything happening within their domain.

Whose Turn Is It to Babysit?
On one of our January safaris, lions seemed to be everywhere. The highlight

Lion cubs play "take down" with mom

came when all three of our vehicles had perfect views of a pride of five lionesses and ten cubs, ranging in age from one to four months. The mothers appeared to be enjoying a well-earned nap while the cubs turned the jade-green meadow into their playground.

The older cubs played a game Julie dubbed "take down ." One would sprint ahead while another launched from behind, tackling the runner to the ground. It was all innocent fun until one cub miscalculated and barreled into a sleeping mother. She swatted at the offender and stood up, triggering delightful chaos.

Suddenly, the game morphed into "Mom, You're the Buffalo and We're the Mighty Hunters." Ten cubs pounced and pranced around her, trying their best to bring her down. One by one, the other lionesses joined in, turning the moment into a full-blown, pride-wide play session. It was a photographer's dream with hours of action, interaction, and joy.

The next morning, Ralph, one of our photographers, declared, "I think I'll stay in today. Yesterday was so perfect—and I need to clean my camera gear."

We returned to the same spot,

Lion cub and disgruntled male

expecting more cub antics. But this time, the cubs were alone. We caught a glimpse of the lionesses disappearing into a grove of trees, off on a hunt. What happens when the mothers leave the cubs behind?

Our question was answered moments later when two massive male lions emerged from the shade and settled near the cubs. Not *with* them—*near* them. These babysitters were clearly not thrilled about their assignment.

Within minutes, one of the cubs sauntered over to the nearest male. As the lion lifted his head and opened his mouth to roar, the youngster leaned in and stuck his head right inside. Another cub approached the second male and pressed his entire body against him. The expressions on the males' faces were priceless—consternation, disbelief, and sheer terror as the cubs came in for a cuddle.

Once again, the cubs stole the show, providing endless entertainment. Back at the lodge, Ralph shook his head and said, "I'm never cleaning my camera gear again."

LIONS IN THE CRATER

In the Ngorongoro Crater, lions thrive despite their confined habitat, with 15-20 prides coexisting. Dominant males fiercely guard their territory, preventing outsiders from entering the Crater. Over time, this leads to inbreeding, genetic stagnation, and the eventual weakening of the lion population. The arrival of new males becomes crucial, as it revitalizes the gene pool and ensures the continued strength of the prides.

Having photographed the Crater over sixty times, I've become familiar with many of its prides. The Munge, the Makuti, the Central, and the Round Top Prides are among the most powerful.

The Munge Pride

On the northeast wall of the Crater flows the Munge River, a stream that is the home territory of the Munge lion pride. Observing this pride has given me priceless opportunities to photograph their complex social structure.

On any typical day, most of the pride will be near the river, with bouncy cubs of all ages swapping blows and biting tails while the adults rest. Distant, deep, thunderous roars from the male lions frequently echo through the valley, summoning the pride to gather.

While a pride's numbers range from twenty to thirty members, it is more common to see smaller groupings. In fact, I had never seen an entire pride all together until one memorable morning when we were near the Munge River. Our driver, Salvatory, suddenly cried, "Look! It's a migration!"

Over a small ridge, the entire Munge Pride—more than thirty lions— was streaming through the grass, moving as a unit to relocate after the previous night's heavy rains. Multiple generations of lions walked together, crossed the Munge River, continued to our road, then flowed around our vehicle, surrounding us in an undulating, tawny ring. It was wondrous and heart-stopping.

Another striking moment involved a zebra kill, its remains serving as both nourishment and entertainment. The adults had had their fill, but the cubs still had energy to burn. The zebra's tail became the centerpiece of a playful game of keep-away among the youngsters, who raced and leapt after the cub flashing the bushy prize.

The game was short-lived, however, lasting only until hyenas arrived. They seized the carcass and engaged in their own scavenger games with the skin, bones, and hooves. This wasn't for me, though some clients wanted to stay. Their Land Cruiser remained with the kill while ours headed to Lake Magadi to see flamingos.

Lioness in full chase mode

Lake Magadi did have flamingos, but, as our driver Nicholas pointed out, there were also three lionesses on the lake shore. They were engaged in unmistakable hunting behavior. It was *Munge Matatu*, three lionesses from the Munge Pride responsible for much of the hunting.

We watched as one of the three lionesses slipped behind us, disappearing far to the left while the other two crouched flat to the ground. Minutes later, hundreds of wildebeest came around a bend in the lake and approached for a drink, stepping into that carefully orchestrated trap. With swift precision, the first lioness revealed herself, triggering a frenzied wildebeest stampede straight into the ambush set by her companions. Lake Magadi's waters exploded with splashing, charging wildebeest. This was another unforgettable testament to the intelligence and resourcefulness of these remarkable predators.

Stick Boy

On our first safari with the children, the Ngorongoro Crater was one of our key destinations. We had yet to familiarize ourselves with the lion prides there, but on our first morning, we encountered the Munge Pride near our lodge. Multiple females and cubs of various ages filled the landscape, playing

The Munge Pride hunting grounds

and wrestling as they moved toward our vehicle.

The children were particularly enchanted by one small male cub who had claimed a sturdy stick as his prized possession. No matter how many times he dropped it, he would snatch it up again, round up his sisters, and race down the hillside with them in pursuit. Despite their best efforts, none could wrestle the stick away. He strutted about triumphantly, stick gripped tightly in his tiny jaws. The girls immediately named him "Stick Boy."

One year later, Stick Boy had grown, now playing keep-away with his eight cousins and sisters, replacing his cherished stick with a set of wildebeest horns. By the third year, those same sisters and cousins had matured into sub-adults. The males were developing impressive manes. We found them in a near-idyllic setting, lounging by the edge of a peaceful pool. Herds of wildebeest and zebra dotted the area, and when a zebra family approached another pool upstream, Stick Boy sprang into action. He circled his cohort, nudging and urging them to join him in a hunt, but none responded. Undeterred, he lifted his head high and marched toward the zebra on a solitary quest.

We couldn't see what unfolded from our vantage point, but we heard the sounds of a sudden stampede and saw the dust cloud rising near the second pool. Stick Boy had made his move. Anticipating a successful hunt, we waited, only for him to emerge from the dust, empty-handed and irritated. As he passed our vehicle, he turned his head slightly, and within moments, we heard the unmistakable *hsss* of a punctured tire. Stick Boy had taken out his frustration on our left rear tire.

Salvatory was livid. "Why didn't you tell me he was going to bite my tire?" he yelled.

We had a flat, surrounded by eight fully grown lions. Without hesitation, Salvatory grabbed a machete from under his seat, jumped out of the vehicle, and changed the tire, cool-headed in the presence of some rather disgruntled big cats.

Years later, on the familiar dirt track leading to the Munge River, the predawn light revealed shifting shapes, jumping, running, advancing toward us. As they grew closer, the shapes took form. Lions!

Salvatory eyed them warily. "Stick Boy's big cubs," he said. "They're trouble."

An unexpected guest

Trouble? How much trouble could lion cubs be? Before I could finish the thought, Salvatory hurriedly rolled up his window as one of the young males made a half-hearted lunge at the vehicle.

"Trouble!" Salvatory repeated, as the cat backed away.

Then, with a single powerful leap, the young lion landed on the hood, his golden eyes locking onto Emma, one of my clients, in the front seat. He pawed at the window, testing it curiously, until Salvatory declared, "I have to move now, before he eats my windshield wipers."

With that, he gunned the engine, surged forward, then reversed, successfully dislodging the inquisitive feline.

Who knows what surprises the next trip to the Munge might bring?

Four Brothers

Years ago, on an early morning expedition, we encountered four large male lions moving together. Every time we approached, they sank into the tall grass. When we backed away, they stood as a unit, watching us. Their matching facial markings revealed them as relatives, but their timid behavior was unusual for Crater lions, who are accustomed to vehicles. We suspected they were newcomers, nervous and unfamiliar with the resident prides. We chose to leave them undisturbed.

Four brothers form a coalition

Four brothers take over the Central Pride

Exactly one year later, we returned and found the Central Pride feasting on a buffalo kill from the previous night. This pride was known for having three strong, dominant males along with many females and cubs. However, to our surprise, four males stood among a pride of twenty-four lions—the four males significantly younger and in their prime. Their facial markings confirmed it: these were the same four males we had encountered a year before. They had successfully integrated, proving that nature has its way of restoring balance.

It's a good feeling of accomplishment when wildlife, natural history, bushcraft, and experience all come together.

SURVIVAL SKILLS

Mating Lions

When lions mate, it's not a brief encounter. It's a week-long marathon. A male and typically one female will leave the pride to find a secluded spot for their honeymoon. Lionesses aren't particularly efficient at conceiving, so success depends on frequent mating. On day one, they mate roughly (pun intended) every eight minutes. On day two, it's every 12 minutes. By the end of the week, hours may pass between sessions.

The ritual begins with the female rising from her rest and circling the male. She then strolls away, glancing back to ensure he follows. When ready, she lowers herself to the ground, and the male mounts her, taking the lead.

The male lion follows the lioness

Biting the female's ear

The final moment

During mating, he gently bites her ear and grips her neck with his powerful jaws.

There's no mistaking the end of the act: the female lets out a fierce growl, spins away, and swipes at the male with her claws. The photographic challenge is to capture that fleeting moment, including the fierce look on the female's face and the male's terrified recoil. As the week progresses, her reactions soften, changing from violent swats to a subtle lip curl and a quiet growl.

A Brilliant Strategy

One morning, while driving near the Munge River, we spotted the pride feasting on a wildebeest kill. But something was off. Two unfamiliar male lions lingered near the scene. Knowing the pride had young cubs, I feared the worst. New males often kill cubs to bring females back into estrus, ensuring their own genes are passed on.

As one male wandered toward a dry riverbed, one of the females began displaying mating behavior

A lioness hides her cubs from a new male

by rolling on the ground and presenting herself. My heart sank. Had the cubs already been killed?

But then, something unexpected happened. Instead of submitting, the lioness crawled away. She stopped about 25 yards off, repeated the display, and again slunk away as he approached. She led him on a slow, deliberate chase, repeating the act until both disappeared over a distant ridge.

"Well, that didn't go how I thought it would," I said. "Let's move on and . . . wait, do you hear that?" It sounded like faint mewing!

We slowly retraced our path toward the dry riverbed. The mews grew louder. Then, from the edge of the gully, a lioness emerged with two tiny cubs in tow.

It all made sense. The pride had been taken over by new males, and the females were protecting their young. While one mother hid her cubs in the safety of the ravine, her sister used a clever distraction—seduction as a decoy—to lure the male far away.

A masterclass in maternal strategy, executed with feline finesse.

A Mother's Protection

In the heart of the Central Serengeti, leopards are often found lounging in the sausage trees that line the Seronera River. These trees offer the perfect vantage point over the river valley, allowing leopards to survey the landscape for prey. Their thick branches serve as secure storage for kills and safe havens for young cubs.

The leopardess brings a gazelle up a tree

Female leopards often leave their cubs nestled high in the canopy while they descend into the grasslands to hunt. One unforgettable morning, we came upon a mother leopard and her two cubs in a magnificent tree, bathed in the golden glow of sunrise. The cubs tumbled and played on the lower branches while their mother silently climbed down to begin her hunt.

A herd of Thomson's gazelles grazed in the tall grass about 100 yards away. We assumed they'd spot her immediately and bolt. I watched the tips of their horns bobbing above the golden tassels, expecting sudden movement. But then, shockingly, a massive leopard paw emerged from the grass and snatched the largest gazelle buck. The grass rippled, then stilled. Moments later, the mother leopard appeared at the base of the tree, the gazelle dangling from her jaws.

In three powerful leaps, she ascended the tree and wedged the kill into a forked branch. But the drama was far from over.

The leopardess scolds her cubs

As she secured the carcass, her cubs scampered down the trunk to play at the tree's base. Suddenly, from behind us, came the unmistakable *woop-woop* of a hyena. The mother froze, eyes locked on the approaching scavenger. The hyena had either seen or smelled the kill and was heading straight for the tree.

The cubs, still on the ground, had hidden themselves in a thicket of bushes. We held our breath. If the hyena caught their scent, it would surely kill them. The mother leopard grew visibly agitated as the hyena reached the base of the tree, sniffing around the area where the cubs had just been playing.

Then, in a stunning act of maternal instinct and strategy, the leopard pulled the gazelle from its perch, dangled it in front of the hyena, and let it drop. The hyena snatched the kill and bolted, instantly forgetting about the cubs.

The mother stood on a low branch and let out a sharp, urgent call. The cubs emerged from the bushes and scrambled up the tree to safety. The expression on the mother's face was fierce and protective, eerily reminiscent of the look my own mother used to give me when I'd pushed her patience too far.

Subterfuge in the Serengeti

In the northern Serengeti, scattered across the plains, are ancient rock formations known as *kopjes,* a word derived from Dutch and Afrikaans meaning "the top of a head." These rocky outcrops are the exposed remnants of long-buried mountains, slowly revealed as the Serengeti Plains took shape. Over thousands of years, erosion split the rocks, allowing trees and shrubs to take root, creating an ideal refuge for leopards.

For leopard cubs, these kopjes offer more than shelter. They offer survival. Hidden in crevices and small caves, the young are largely protected from predators. But among all threats, lions pose the greatest danger. Territorial and intolerant of rival big cats, lions will chase off adult leopards and kill their cubs to eliminate competition.

One dry season, we discovered a leopard den tucked into a remote kopje far from our camp. Each morning, we'd rise early, drive out, and park a respectful hundred meters away to observe without intruding.

The leopardess runs back to her hidden cubs

One day, we arrived just in time to see the mother leopard emerge. She scanned the area cautiously, then proceeded down the slope to a nearby stream. We watched her drink, and drink, and drink. It went on far longer than usual. Why would she need so much water?

When she finally finished, she didn't return directly to the den. Instead, she veered left, marking a bush with urine. Then she continued past the den, keeping her distance, and marked another bush. She kept walking, spraying bushes every fifty yards until she disappeared over a ridge.

We returned to our vantage point, puzzled but intrigued. About thirty minutes later, we spotted her in the distance, sprinting toward the den. She ran full tilt for over a mile and dove into the cave. All we could see were two pale eyes glinting from the shadows.

Then came the answer to our mystery.

A massive lioness appeared, padding up the hill with laser focus on the leopard's den. We braced ourselves for a dramatic confrontation. But instead of charging, the lioness paused and sniffed the ground

A lioness searches for the leopard cubs

where the leopard had left her scent. She turned away from the den and followed the trail of markings, stopping every fifty yards to sniff until she too vanished over the ridge.

The mother leopard had sensed the lioness's approach. She drank deeply to produce enough urine, then laid a false trail, leading the lioness away from her cubs. Her cunning had saved them from certain death.

THE GREAT MIGRATION

Each February, the great migration of wildebeest, zebras, and gazelles sweeps into the short grass plains of the Southern Serengeti. Triggered by the November rains, the fresh growth provides vital nutrients for nursing wildebeest mothers, essential for the healthy milk their calves depend on. My safari schedule is usually timed perfectly to witness this miracle of life.

But witnessing a wildebeest birth is no easy feat. Filming one is exponentially harder. Most births occur between 9 and 11 a.m., as the day begins to warm. With millions of animals spread across the plains, finding the one about to give birth is like searching for a needle in one hundred haystacks. Our strategy is to drive slowly through the herds, scanning for

Wildebeest herds invade the plains

females that look uncomfortable or are lying on their sides, pushing. But get too close, and she'll retreat into the safety of the herd. It's easy to lose them in the endless sea of movement.

Once labor begins, tiny hooves and legs emerge from the birth canal, making it easier to track the mother. But another complication lurks: hyenas. They follow the herds, waiting for vulnerable newborns. Wildebeest have evolved a remarkable defense. They can delay birth for up to two weeks if predators are nearby. My son Anders has a saying:

"If you are a wildebeest mom and you want a successful birth, make sure every hyena has a wildebeest calf in its mouth. Then give birth. All will be well."

The Perfect Wildebeest Birth

During filming for *To the Ends of the Earth: East Africa*, capturing a wildebeest birth was the key to the project's success. I had a full month in Tanzania, with 20 days in the heart of the birthing grounds. It should've been easy.

But the short rains never came. For two weeks, the Serengeti remained dry. Our backup location, the Ngorongoro Crater—home to its own resident herds—was just as barren. No rain, no births.

Then, hope. There were reports of rain in the Serengeti! A few days later, we returned to find lush green grass. But, to our dismay, there were thousands of baby wildebeest already born, nursing, and resting in nursery groups. We had missed the birthing window by mere days. Our final chance was the Crater.

The first two days showed promise—just a few newborns, meaning births were still possible. But the skies stayed clear, and no births came.

It was our last day. Four weeks in, and not a single birth filmed. It had rained the night before, so we had hope. A precious three hours remained before we had to exit the Crater and drive to Arusha for our flight home. I drove with a gifted young photographer named Ashleigh and with Joe, who always had two large mugs of coffee every morning.

As we neared the Crater's birthing grounds, Two Cups Joe called from the back, "Hey, can we take a bathroom break?" In the Crater, you can't just step out; you have to drive to a designated picnic area, taking a 20-minute detour.

We went to the picnic site, and time slipped away. In my mind, I could see a cartoon clock with its hands spinning faster and faster. Then, just as we were about to escape the picnic site, Ashleigh squealed, "Monkeys!" Six vervet monkeys perched in an acacia tree. I sighed, feeling the entire birthing project fade, along with all my hopes and dreams.

We finally finished with the monkeys. My hopes and dreams had revived, and we proceeded to the birthing grounds. There weren't many wildebeest out there—just a few stragglers near the road. Once again, my hopes and dreams were fading. When all seemed lost, our guide Salvatory burst out, "She's giving birth!"

A wildebeest stood and dropped a calf right in front of us. Was I excited? Absolutely. Was I ready? Not even close.

But before I could panic, Salva shouted again, "It's another one! She's standing!"

I didn't hesitate. I grabbed my camera rig, set it on the roof, and repeated my mantra, *Don't panic. Don't panic.*

Through the camera, she was perfectly framed—just the right distance for my 600mm lens. I hit record. She began to spin, revealing the legs. Then, with a perfect turn, the head, neck, and torso emerged. I checked the red light;

A wildebeest gives birth

Mother and calf bonding

yes, I was filming. She spun again. The calf, halfway out, kicked its hooves and looked around. Then, with a dramatic *whoosh*, the amniotic fluid and the entire calf spilled onto the ground.

I could barely breathe. The mother turned, licked away the placenta, and nudged the calf to nurse. In that five-minute window, the success of the entire month was sealed.

As I sat in awe, replaying the moment in my mind, I heard Ashleigh say from the back of the van, "Todd, are you crying?"

I paused. *Yes. I was.*

TARANGIRE NATIONAL PARK

Tarangire National Park in Tanzania is known for its towering baobab trees, dense elephant populations, and an impressive variety of bush birds. Wildlife numbers fluctuate with the seasons, shifting with the rains that affect which species appear in the park.

During the wet season, the soil becomes sticky, clinging to hooves and leading to disease. As a result, zebras, giraffes, and other hoofed animals migrate

Elephants in the marsh

Baobab trees

Making a path through the reeds

to the wilderness outside the park, where the terrain is firmer and safer.

Elephants, however, thrive in the rainy season. The massive marsh at the southern end of the park fills with water, sprouting fresh grasses and reeds. Herds wade through the shallows to feed, while others plunge into ponds for a swim. The largest females use their tusks to clear pathways through dense marsh grasses for their calves.

The Big Marsh

One particularly unforgettable afternoon, our vehicle followed a track skirting the marsh. A few African white pelicans flew by, then more, then even more. As we approached, we realized they were landing just ahead. By the time we reached the open pond, thousands of pelicans had gathered, dipping their heads in synchronized motions—a breathtaking display of coordinated feeding. There must have been a massive fish hatching, the spectacle unfolding right before us.

Fishing pelicans

Another year, heavy rains transformed the marsh into a feeding ground for saddle-billed storks. Some trips yield just one or two sightings of these massive, colorful birds, and in other years, none at all. But this time, scores of them lined the water's edge. Their battles with enormous catfish emerging from hibernation were intense, each stork struggling to subdue its slippery opponent. One determined catfish managed to escape a saddle-billed-stork— only to be scooped up moments later by an African fish eagle.

Leopards occasionally make an appearance, along with lions, and on two memorable occasions, wild dogs.

All this sets the backdrop for what happened next.

A Tortoise and Quicksand

This particular year, the short rains never arrived, and the dry season stretched on. I drove with two friends, Jim and Roger. Wildlife sightings were sparse—a few zebras and a lone warthog. Our driver, James, tirelessly scouted the park for something interesting, but it felt empty. We scoured vast areas, moving north to south, and sweeping the width of Tarangire. Still nothing.

Eventually, we crossed out of the park, entering the wilderness beyond. The landscape slowly changed, revealing new terrain. We came upon a sand river that I had never seen before. We followed it for a few kilometers until Roger suddenly shouted, "Stop!" We looked around, but nothing obvious caught our attention. Roger pointed across the dry riverbed at a huge, flat rock. There, at eye level, stood a leopard tortoise. On any other day, we would have driven by without much thought. But today? It felt like we'd found the pot of gold at the end of the rainbow.

We asked James if we could step out to photograph the tortoise. After checking for lions, James confirmed it was fine. Roger asked, "Why check for lions if there aren't any animals within a hundred miles?"

Leopard tortoise

Jim is a meticulous photographer, taking his time to ensure every equipment detail is perfect before going for a shot. Roger and I, on the other hand, grabbed our macro lenses and bolted out the door in seconds. We crossed the sand to the flat rock and photographed the tortoise at eye level. It was fascinating to see the space between its heavy shell and the rock beneath it.

Roger and I had already returned to the vehicle when Jim finally started crossing the sand to take his shot. Moments later, we heard him shout, "Oh, no!" We turned to see Jim sinking into quicksand. He had chosen a different path across and had unknowingly stepped into a hidden sinkhole. He was going down fast, just like the kid in *Lawrence of Arabia*.

Jim was waist-deep, frantically holding his camera gear above his head and pleading, "At least save this!" Roger grabbed the camera while James and I pulled him up by the arms. It took real effort, but we managed to drag him out. Instead of gasping in relief or thanking us, Jim simply stated, "I think one of my sandals is still down there. Could you get it for me?"

That sent us into another round of hysterical laughter. James, ever patient, reached into the sinkhole and retrieved the sandal.

The drive back took a while, mostly because we couldn't stop laughing. Jim casually asked if we could share the story with the rest of the group. Mid-laugh, James suddenly turned serious.

"Absolutely not."

The statute of limitations on this story has officially run out.

CHEETAH VALLEY

People often ask if I'm afraid of wild animals when I'm out filming in the most remote places on earth. They ask:

"Have you had any close calls?"

"Aren't you always in danger?"

"Have you ever feared for your life?"

And my answer, every time, is a solid, "No."

I've never had a dramatic brush with a predator. The truth is, when I've

Cheetah Valley

been hurt—and I have—it's always been my own doing. Mishaps are part of the job. What really matters is how you handle them, and how far you are from medical help when they happen.

In Northern Serengeti, the main show is the great migration, the dramatic crossings of the Mara River. If the rains come, the wildebeest move to new grass. If rain doesn't come, the herds don't cross. On those dry days, we veer off the predictable routes to search for other animals. Driving out of the river valley will bring us to kopjes, weather-worn remnants of volcanic mountains that are home to leopards.

Further on is a place the guides call Cheetah Valley. It's the Serengeti at its most cinematic. The sweeping golden valleys, towering plateaus, and acacia trees are spaced so perfectly, you'd swear it was designed by a landscape artist. It's home to everything—lions, giraffes, elephant families, topi, impala, and even the elusive serval cat. But the real action happens when cheetahs are hunting.

Male cheetahs often form coalitions—tight-knit brothers-in-arms—and when they hunt together, it's something to behold.

One evening, we found ourselves in the middle of pure chaos: wildebeest racing in every direction, thousands of them, storming through the tawny grass and under umbrella acacia trees.

"Cheetahs," our guide Peter said, pointing ahead.

I stood up and looked through the roof hatch to get a better view as we crept through the mass of galloping animals. Eventually, we spotted the source of the stampede. There were three male cheetahs, weaving through the herds. At first, they seemed half-committed, darting left and right like

Hunting cheetah

they couldn't agree on a plan. But in reality, they were testing the herds, looking for weakness. Suddenly, they found it—an injured calf.

The cheetahs took off. We accelerated, too, not wanting to lose the moment. I was still standing upright in the Land Rover, and that's when it happened. Wham! The rear tire dropped into an aardvark hole. The impact launched me skyward, my body propelled three feet higher than the roof hatch. As I came down, the vehicle came up. The vehicle and I met midair. I blacked out.

When I opened my eyes, I was lying on the floor of the vehicle, staring up through the roof hatch with tears streaming down my cheeks. The pain in my back was agonizing. It felt like I'd been speared with a hot poker. It drilled deeper with any movement. Getting into a seat, I might as well have been scaling Everest. The interminable drive back to camp was excruciating torture, but leaving the jeep was even worse. I couldn't support myself or move my legs. When I picked up a branch to use as a crutch, I nearly fainted.

That night, I had dinner with the group whose average age had to be near 75. Their consensus, based on decades of personal orthopedic wisdom, was that I had a compressed disc. Fortunately, the team was also a walking pharmacy, and I was soon loaded up with enough anti-inflammatory drugs and pain killers to tranquilize an angry buffalo.

I hobbled through the rest of the safari. It took five years for my spine to fully heal.

But to this day, I've never had a dangerous encounter with a wild animal. Just an unlucky run-in with an aardvark hole.

NAMIBIA

Namibia is a photographer's dream. Its desert landscapes are masterpieces of color and texture, offering infinite possibilities for capturing stunning images. Towering dunes, volcanic terrains, and rugged mountains provide a dramatic backdrop. And Namibia's wildlife is just as extraordinary.

Along the Skeleton Coast, colonies of Cape fur seals, numbering in the hundreds of thousands, claim the shores. Desert elephants roam the dunes alongside oryx and springbok. But the crown jewel of Namibia's wildlife game parks is the legendary Etosha National Park, a vast expanse teeming with lions, southern giraffes, springbok, black rhino, oryx, and the world's largest elephants.

Wildlife photography in Namibia differs from photography in East Africa. In Tanzania and Kenya, animals are seemingly everywhere. You drive, find them, and photograph them. But in the Namibian desert, survival depends on water. The key to great photography is understanding when and where different species arrive at the waterholes.

For example, if elephants are spotted in the distance but roads won't take you to them, the smartest move is to stake out the nearest waterhole. Eventually, they'll come. If they seem to be moving away, odds are they've already had their drink, and it's best to move to another location.

The Oryx vs. the Honey Badger
One picturesque watering hole in Etosha is particularly productive, where anything can happen. As always, early mornings and late afternoons are prime hours for wildlife activity.

On this afternoon, nothing remarkable seemed to be happening. Yet, the atmosphere felt off. Springbok twitched nervously. An old oryx hesitated before kneeling to drink. Jackals lurked, nipping at each other as they circled the watering hole. A massive kori bustard, the world's heaviest flying bird, strode into the scene, puffing up in a threat display to push the springbok away. Zebras appeared but didn't stay for long.

Then, across the rocky terrain, a lone figure emerged, a shape I couldn't quite recognize. It moved fast, sprinting toward the watering hole with an oddly hunched gait.

A giant mongoose? Too bulky. An African wild cat? Too bold. As it came closer, it revealed itself—a honey badger, the fiercest little terror in all of Africa!

At the honey badger's approach, the watering hole cleared instantly. Every animal scattered except for the lone oryx. He rose from his knees, locking eyes with the newcomer. The honey badger's stance was unmistakable. This waterhole was his, and he wanted everyone to know it.

What happened next was incredible. The honey badger charged, teeth bared, fur bristling. The oryx stepped back, then slammed the badger into the rocky ground with his scimitar-like horns! The badger, wounded but defiant, dragged himself back to the watering hole, mixing dirt and water, creating mud to plaster over his injuries, a natural armor against infection.

Then, unbelievably, he charged again. This time, the massive antelope lowered his horns, scooped him up, and flung him thirty yards through the air, sending him crashing to the ground in a cloud of dust! The battle was won, and the oryx turned and walked away.

But the chaos wasn't over yet. The badger staggered back toward the waterhole, determined to drink after his epic fight. I was set up with my 1200mm lens, hoping for a close-up. With such a narrow field of view, I nearly missed what happened next.

On the edge of the frame, a shadow crept close to the badger. Switching to a shorter lens, I barely caught the moment. It was a jackal sneaking up behind the drinking badger. With a flash of teeth, the jackal nipped his foot. In an instant, teeth flashed, fur flew, and bodies twisted as the two battled.

Then another jackal joined the fray. Then another.

An oryx tosses a honey badger

A jackal challenges a honey badger

And another. Hyenas entered the scene, and the battle rolled behind us into the open desert. By the time the melee ended, three hyenas and four jackals had failed to take down the honey badger. One hyena didn't survive, and the rest fled into the wilderness. The badger, undefeated, returned to the watering hole and calmly finished his drink.

We finally caught our breath. As the sun dipped lower, I turned to my crew and sighed.

"Oh my God. Nothing could top that."

The words had barely left my mouth when our driver and guide, Dirk, whispered, "Lions." We turned—and there, in the last golden light of the dying day, were five big lionesses.

I switched gears, setting up my shot to capture the empty watering hole before they arrived. With slow, confident strides, they made their way to the pool. One lioness crested the ridge and dipped her head to drink. Then another. Then another. One by one, five queens of the desert lined the pool's edge, drinking in perfect symmetry. After getting enough video, I switched to still photography just in time to capture one lioness staring straight into my lens. Moments later, they stretched, turned, and disappeared into the fading light.

Lions in golden light drink at the water hole

Pangolins

Pangolins are nocturnal, scaly anteaters that are the most trafficked animal in the world, currently red-listed as endangered by the IUCN. They are so rare that I have never seen one in all my decades of safari travel.

In 2023, I arranged to visit a protected reserve in Namibia where pangolins might be found. It is enclosed by security fencing and patrolled by rangers to prevent poaching. The reserve also has cheetahs, leopards, giraffes, and zebras, so we would have plenty to see if we didn't find a pangolin.

Sean and Gerry, a lovely couple originally from Ireland, accompanied me on this mission. Our first outing also included two other tourists. The guide drove the five of us through the reserve, stopping at various animals. He then spotted a leopard. It walked out of the bush, lay down in a muddy ditch, and went to sleep.

While we watched this riveting wildlife spectacle, word came over the radio that a pangolin had been spotted in a different part of the reserve. The driver asked if we wanted to go there.

Sean, Gerry, and I gave a resounding, "Yes!"

The other two in the van said, "Absolutely not. We came for leopards, and there's one right in front of us."

So, we stayed and watched the sleeping leopard. After five long minutes, and with the sun low in the west, the tourists said they had seen enough, and we could leave.

We thanked them and cried, "Let's go!" to the driver. His response was to make a careful seventeen-point turn, ratchet the jeep into first gear, and rocket away at a cautious five mph.

Eventually, we arrived at the other side of the reserve. My pre-visualization had been to photograph the pangolin at a low angle with nothing behind him. I had my 600mm lens ready to go. Well, the pangolin was in tall grass and had other plans. The only way to photograph him was to be very close and to look down through the grass. I knew the shoot was a disaster when the only clear shot I had was of the pangolin walking between Sean's legs.

That night, I went through possible scenarios assuming we would have another chance with this amazing animal. If we could only photograph the pangolin from close-up, I would try to use my "Turtle-Cam 2000" (named as an homage to Harry Potter's flying broom), which I designed and have used to film baby sea turtles at ground level.

The next day, we told our guide that we would like, if possible, to be the only people in the jeep. We didn't need to see leopards, and we could wait at the lodge until the pangolin was sighted. That way, we could quickly go directly to the pangolin.

At three o'clock, we got the word: the pangolin was out! We piled into the jeep, and our guide once again sped along at five mph. The sun was sinking behind the mountains by the time we arrived.

The pangolin wandered through a meadow that was mostly clear of tall grass. I grabbed the Turtle-Cam 2000 and was able to film the pangolin at eye level from about two feet away. A pangolin can roll into an impenetrable ball if disturbed, and I was careful to stay out of its way. He walked to a clearing, climbed a small termite hill, went in one of the holes to feed, then circled the whole mound.

As I filmed, I heard the ranger say, "He's heading for the road!"

This would be the chance for me to get my dreamed-of long lens shot with a clear background. I looked for the jeep, but it was now 100 meters away! I would never make it in time.

As I started running back, I heard Gerry yell, "I got your back, Boy-o!"

And there she was, running toward me with my 600mm lens. About 10 feet away, her foot caught a rock, and as she fell forward, she threw the lens. It flew into my waiting arms. It was exactly like the scene in *The Patriot* when René Auberjonois throws the loaded rifle to Heath Ledger. I dropped to the

Pangolin at eye level

ground, focused, and began filming the pangolin.

What an extraordinary experience!

UGANDA KOB

Of all the mating rituals I've observed in the wild, few are as elaborate and scripted as that of the Uganda kob. With their golden to reddish-brown coats, white chest patches, and distinct eye rings, they look like a mash-up between a waterbuck and an impala.

During a day off from gorilla trekking, we detoured to Uganda's Queen Elizabeth National Park, famous for its lakes and tree-climbing lions. For our first photo activity, we had scheduled a boat tour on a 30-foot vessel where the first deck was twelve feet above the waterline. The tour over the lakes had its moments. There were plenty of birds and wildlife, but I've never been a fan of high-decked boats, where you're perpetually shooting down at the action like a bird-watcher on stilts. We soon ditched the lake and set off in search of lions. We didn't find them. But we did find something even more memorable.

Years ago, I'd read *The Safari Companion* by Richard Estes, the definitive text on African wildlife behavior. In it, Estes chronicles the behaviors of almost every animal in East Africa, including the Uganda kob. Despite having never seen one, I instantly recognized a Uganda kob on the horizon. My

Uganda kob whistling

Uganda kob mating

fervent hope was that this would be the time of mating. As we approached, the scene unfolded into a spellbinding mating ritual. Ten male kobs had spaced themselves evenly into a vast circle, each buck about a hundred yards apart—a classic lek. Each male staked out a position and emitted a piercing whistle, exactly like an elk.

At some unknown cue, a single female stepped into the ring. One male moved to intercept her. If his attempt to mate failed, he quietly retreated to his post, and the next suitor took a turn. Round after round, male after male, the ritual played out in the dry golden grass with whistles marking the courtship's rhythm.

But then came a twist. A young female entered the circle with a distinct air, head high and confident. The males didn't whistle. They shuffled. They pawed the ground. And then, unexpectedly, two of them broke formation and drove her out of the arena. She wasn't of age.

I'd never seen anything like it. But thanks to one very dog-eared field guide, I recognized the setup and caught the story unfolding in real time . . . because sometimes, the best camera trick is *just knowing what to look for.*

MOUNTAIN GORILLAS

Only three countries can claim populations of wild mountain gorillas: the Democratic Republic of Congo, Rwanda, and Uganda. I've trekked 34 times through the jungles of Rwanda and Uganda, and no two encounters have ever been alike. That's because three major factors shape each experience: family dynamics, time of day, and habitat.

Every gorilla family has its own social rhythm. A typical group includes a dominant silverback, adult females, adolescents, juveniles, and babies. Some families have multiple infants; others have more than one silverback. Each configuration brings its own mood and its own challenges when you're filming.

Gorilla brother and sister share babysitting in an open green glade

Then there's timing. Mountain gorillas divide their days into sleep, play, feeding, rest, traveling, nest-building, and more sleep. The window you arrive in determines whether you see a slow-motion brunch or a full-on jungle gym free-for-all.

Finally, the habitat shapes everything. Ancient forests with towering old-growth trees offer dramatic views of gorillas climbing, playing, and swinging from vines. Younger forests have open glades where the light spills across green shrubs—ideal for watching them forage and wrestle. And then there's bamboo. It's beautiful, but a nightmare to shoot in. Light slicing through the stalks throws bright highlights that wash out their dark fur. And there are distracting pale, dead leaves.

All this is to set the stage for what happened in the gorilla treks that follow.

Bwindi Impenetrable Forest

It was my very first gorilla trek, and I soon found that Uganda's Bwindi Impenetrable Forest is no joke. It is simply dense, ancient jungle with trails that vanish if you blink. It contains thorns that grab, nettles that sting straight through shirts and socks, and terrain that tests even the fittest hikers.

We started late. One of the eight in our group forgot his camera batteries. He needed a break every few hundred yards, then decided to "see Africa" and got lost. By the time we reached the glade—an extraordinary grove of old-

Bwindi Impenetrable Forest

growth trees perfect for filming—the gorillas were having none of it. They descended from the canopy and marched off at double-time.

We'd missed everything. After having already woken, played, eaten, and rested, they were off again in search of a new nesting spot. What should have been a leisurely 45-minute trek turned into a six-hour marathon. We never reached the family before they disappeared into the trees for the night.

Exhausted, we began the long trek back. I was shot, both physically and mentally. The forest's ups and downs felt endless. But there was a kid in our group, a mountain climber from Aspen, wearing a red jacket. He became my beacon. I just focused on his coat, trying to keep up. He always seemed just out of reach, over the next rise or down the next ravine. At one point, desperate for rest, I leaned against a skinny tree on the only small, flat patch of ground I could find—maybe six inches wide—hoping to catch my breath.

And that's when I heard it: "Come, Mr. Frodo. I can't carry it for you, but I can carry you!" I looked up. It was the kid from Aspen. That unexpected *Lord of the Rings* quote? It was a shot of adrenaline. I laughed. Then I hiked on.

Eye to Eye with a Giant

If trekking in Uganda tests your mettle, Rwanda offers a gentler climb. The trails are shorter, the terrain more forgiving. And sometimes, gorillas come to you.

Our easiest trek ever began with a hike through potato fields to the buffalo wall. This barrier, made of piled volcanic rock, separates farmers' fields from the dense forests that are the gorillas' home. Our guide paused. "The trackers are on the move with our assigned gorilla family," he said. "Best to wait before plunging into the forest."

"We'll know the direction soon," he assured us. We walked a bit farther along the wall. Another pause. Another call on the radio. "Still waiting," he said.

Before anyone could lift a boot, the forest delivered. Twenty-three gorillas climbed over the buffalo wall and strolled up the slope toward us. The light was gentle, dreamy. A silverback strode along with a young one. Three

Eye to eye with a silverback

other silverbacks vaulted the wall, then paraded past. Some clambered into trees, others tumbled down the hillside in bursts of play. But the moment that stuck with me was when the dominant silverback lumbered toward me on all fours, settled onto the ground, and locked eyes with mine. We shared a long, quiet stare before he moved on.

Big Ben and the Bamboo

And then there's Big Ben, a one-of-a-kind character and the only bald male gorilla I've ever encountered. Not exactly cover shot material. Most photographers turn their lenses elsewhere. But Ben? He's got a soft spot for babies. Anytime a gorilla mother needs a break, her youngster will find Ben, who's always up for a tumble or chase. He's the babysitter everyone wishes they had.

On this trip, I had a guide who hadn't worked with me before. He was enthusiastic but clearly unfamiliar with what I needed for photography. His goal was to find gorillas for us. Mission accomplished. The family was resting in a bamboo glade—my least favorite setting. Harsh beams of sunlight slashed through the stalks, washing out every detail of their jet-black fur. I climbed

Big Ben and his babysitting duties

a small berm beside the glade and tried explaining how tough this light was. The guide simply shrugged. "I found you gorillas," he said. Fair point.

I let out an aggravated sigh and threw my hands in the air. That's when I felt it: a heavy hand on my shoulder. I turned. Right beside me sat Big Ben. He patted my arm as if to say, *I get it, man. I've been there. It's gonna be alright.* And in that instant, I realized that if this guy could walk around bald in a world obsessed with glamour shots and still chase baby gorillas with pure joy, what did I have to complain about?

High Bogs and Silverbacks

One of our treks took us into the high mountain bogs, skirting stands of bamboo. My guide on this trip knew me from past journeys. He understood what I needed to make a photograph sing. As we emerged from the bamboo into an open glade, I could already tell the light was brutal. Harsh sun carved sharp shadows across the gorillas' dark fur. They played and fed in short green grass, but situationally, it was a mess.

Sensing my disappointment, the guide quietly placed a hand on my shoulder and led me to the meadows where the light was slightly better. "A little farther," he whispered.

And it would have worked if I hadn't walked straight into a grass-covered bog and dropped three feet down. I had mud, water, and floating grass up to my waist and couldn't climb out while holding my cameras out of the sludgy water. My guide was completely incapacitated with laughter. I had to admit it was funny, watching the gorillas troop past while I was half-buried and doing my best impersonation of Wile E. Coyote in quicksand. Now I know how Jim felt when he was trapped by quicksand in Tarangire. Falling into holes seems to be a frequent hazard for nature photographers.

Once he regained composure and hauled me out, he leaned in and said, "It's okay. There's another meadow just beyond the bamboo. Let's circle ahead."

We slipped around the grove and reached the clearing just as the family emerged. It was spectacular! Fourteen gorillas strode across the open meadow like they owned it. The light was perfect. The largest silverback stopped mid-step, held his head high, and posed like a movie star against an idyllic background of verdant forest, puffy clouds, and blue mountain sky.

I was still catching my breath when he lumbered over, collapsed at my feet, rolled onto his back, and fell asleep.

But the babies weren't resting. They tumbled into the glade, not walking so much as rolling across the meadow with gleeful abandon. Everyone watched, grinning, lost in the moment, when I suddenly felt something press against my shoulder.

The silverback had stirred, hungry, and now was leaning on me. He propped his elbow on my shoulder like I was a tree stump, while reaching for a patch of tender bamboo just above my head.

I froze, glanced around for help. But no one noticed. They were all photographing the baby gorillas. By the time anyone looked, the silverback was back on all fours and I quietly slunk away.

A silverback asleep at my feet

58

Julie and the Silverback

On another eventful gorilla trek in Rwanda's Virunga Mountains, our group had made a special request. We wanted a gorilla family feeding in an open, green habitat, and a big silverback for good measure. Julie even joked that she needed photographic proof for friends back home, saying, "I would love a photo of me with a silverback in the background."

The guides were happy to oblige. Soon, we left the potato fields behind, crossed the buffalo wall, and entered a corridor of bamboo. That stretch had always made me uneasy with its limited view and shifting shadows, but we passed through without incident. We pressed on through thick saplings and dense underbrush until the trail suddenly tipped upward, leading us into a sun-drenched chain of open glades, flush with nettles, shrubs, and knee-high grass.

And there they were—gorillas, quietly feeding.

It was hard to tell how many at first. The glades were divided by small thickets and saplings, creating pockets of activity. But our guides knew the family and confirmed it: twenty-one gorillas surrounded us. We moved quietly through the greenery. Mothers cradled sleepy infants, and juveniles tumbled down hillsides while adolescents wrestled. The older ones sat apart, focused on breakfast. It felt like we were walking through an ancient, leafy cathedral.

A silver-haired beauty and a silverback

Eventually, we found the silverback. Massive and serene, he sat at the far edge of a clearing, stripping and eating nettles with practiced ease as he kept watch over his family.

"This is it," I whispered to Julie. "He's the one. It's a photo op of a lifetime. Just kneel there, same level as him . . . now slide back . . . a tiny bit more."

Julie looked unsure. "Relax," I said. "He's totally calm. He's just eating." I raised the camera. *Click*. I got one shot before the silverback rose onto all fours, his gaze fixed firmly on Julie. She must've seen something in my expression because she asked, "What's wrong?" I didn't answer. I was too busy watching 500 pounds of muscle pivot and start walking straight toward her with a purposeful stride.

Let me pause here to offer two cardinal rules of gorilla trekking:

1. Don't point at a gorilla.
2. Never, ever run from a gorilla.

Julie stood up, pointed at the gorilla, and, channeling pure Scooby-Doo panic, *Deedle-deedle-deedle-deedle-deedle—P-Kooo!* sprinting toward the guides in a little cloud of dust, with a fired-up silverback close behind. The guides, the trackers, and I formed a protective huddle around her as the silverback circled us, determined, scanning for a gap. I think it must have been Julie's silver hair that attracted him. He paced, huffed, and circled again. Then, just as suddenly, he lost interest and slipped back into the green.

"I think he's faking it. He's trying to lure me out." Julie whispered. "It's a trap."

She stayed in the safety of the group until our hour with the gorillas ended and we began the descent down the mountain. The photo with the silverback will forever be a reminder of this adventure in the Virunga Mountains.

Anders and the Mountain

The primary goal of this expedition was to film gorilla behavior for *The Natural World* documentary. The mission was multi-layered. It included audio recordings in Tanzania for the upcoming *Birds of East Africa* documentary, and delivering a Museum Edition of my book set to the Cultural Heritage Centre. My son Anders joined me on this trip as the sound recording tech, stepping into a project and its sprawling itinerary that had no shortage of moving parts.

We had designed custom-built flight cases to protect the 90-pound book set. This custom edition was bound in weathered dhow sailcloth, bearing hand-stitched leather title cartouches. His Holiness Pope Francis himself viewed the set and said, "With these books you have the power to change hearts and minds and make this a better world." No pressure, right?

After Tanzania, we headed to Rwanda for two days of gorilla trekking. I was especially eager to see it through Anders's eyes. Day one was solid, if unspectacular. But day two—*that* was a trek for the ages.

Anders had no issue with elevation. At over 11,000 feet, he bounded ahead like a mountain goat while I, for reasons unknown, felt completely drained. My pace slowed, my frustration grew, and it all came to a head when I slipped on a narrow trail. Instinctively grabbing for support, I sliced my hand on a jagged bamboo stalk, one that had clearly been angle-cut by a guide's machete. I may have let a few words fly as I tore it down.

And that's when a sub-adult female gorilla's face appeared. She had been crouched just beyond the bamboo, neither of us ready for the other. I screamed. She screamed. I fell backward into a bush. She bolted. It was mutual hysteria.

The guide, clearly surprised, admitted they hadn't known any gorillas were in that sector. We moved on and linked up with the trackers, who gestured across a fallen stand of bamboo toward an open hillside. It was time to approach. According to protocol, we could only take our cameras. Our walking sticks had to be left behind because gorillas could mistake them for spears.

That's when the real trouble started.

The fallen bamboo formed what looked like a solid bridge, thirty feet above the forest floor. I took a few steps. The stalks were slick, and I had no walking stick for balance. I slipped and fell the full thirty feet to the ground, landing flat on my back. The entire trekking group stared down, some in horror, some with concern, some in barely-contained amusement. And Anders? My loving, loyal son? He was doubled over, helpless with laughter, tears in his eyes. To his credit, he did climb down and help pull me up.

Thankfully, the gorilla encounter that followed made it all worthwhile. A mother cradled her newborn, a silverback delivered a series of threat displays, and Anders caught crisp, clean audio from the hillside. Trek complete.

Back in Kigali, we retrieved the books' flight cases, flew to Amsterdam, and rented a car to meet Julie in Bruges, where she'd just completed a bike-and-barge trip. Two friends arrived from England, our daughter flew in from Chicago, and suddenly, we had a full complement of storytellers.

A silverback's threat display

But those tales? That's a story for another day.

Years later, I'm proud to say these treks have helped make a difference. The visibility that tourism brings protects the gorillas. It puts more eyes on the forest and more dollars into conservation. Proceeds help build and maintain the buffalo wall, reducing gorilla-human conflict. Former poachers are now guides and porters. Most importantly, trained trackers spend their days shadowing the gorilla families, deterring poaching and helping tourists connect safely with these magnificent creatures.

When I began trekking, there were only 704 mountain gorillas in the wild. Now, thanks to these combined efforts, there are over 1060. That's not just progress. It's a profound conservation win.

CHASING NORTH AMERICA'S GIANTS

Most of my photographic adventures take me to distant lands—Tanzania, Namibia, Rwanda, Madagascar, India, Costa Rica, Brazil, and other tropical destinations. Yet North America holds wild places that, for those unfamiliar, might feel like the ends of the earth. A few years ago, I decided to turn my lens toward those untamed landscapes, seeking North American ungulates—mule deer, bighorn sheep, musk ox, bison, pronghorns, elk, and especially moose.

The best moose habitats seemed to be out west, where two distinct species caught my attention: Shiras moose and Alaskan moose.

The Search for Alaskan Moose

The Alaska-Yukon moose (*Alces alces gigas*) is the largest moose species. With my photo gear in tow, I set off for Alaska, hoping to capture musk ox and caribou in the far north, and moose near Anchorage.

Moose turned up in various places, but the best location we found was just outside Anchorage in an area fittingly nicknamed "The Moose Bowl."

We arrived and unpacked our gear. I had visited Anchorage years before in summer and recalled the breathtaking view from the car park's edge. But this time, it was the cusp of winter, and snow dusted everything in the valley.

My friend and Alaskan resident, Nick, scanned the vast bowl, pointing out moose that only his trained eye could detect. A bull moose was browsing on the right side, but no trail led near him. A female and calf, visible straight ahead, were disappearing over the ridge.

Nick focused on an area where three hikers stood motionless. Based on his experience, he suspected they had just watched moose feeding, and the animals were now resting. By the time we reached them, the moose would likely be up and grazing again.

As we approached the trailhead at the base of the parking area, two hikers rushed toward us, wide-eyed and panting. One asked, "Did you see the moose?"

"Oh yeah, we spotted one across the valley," I replied casually.

"No! I mean that one!" the hiker exclaimed, pointing over his shoulder to where a massive bull moose rounded a bend in the trail and headed straight toward us.

I had my 600mm telephoto lens on. It was far too large for the close-up encounter barreling toward us. Quickly, I switched to a 400mm lens and considered moving ahead for a dramatic angle. That thought lasted all of half a second before reality hit—I was not stepping in front of him.

Instead, I filmed him as he moved along the precipice, his massive antlers framed by the stunning valley backdrop. He was the largest moose I had ever seen. Side note: This was the first moose I had ever seen up close. I turned to Nick. He gave me a slow nod and said simply, "A pity he's so young. He might grow bigger antlers in a few years."

"What?" My brain short-circuited. Nick explained that this bull's antlers were only 60 inches across. "Yeah? So?" I asked, still dumbfounded.

"The ones we're hoping to film have 96-100-inch antlers," he replied.

I couldn't even imagine it. As we hiked deeper into the valley, I kept calculating. What lens would I need to capture an animal that large? What distance would be optimal?

We passed towering boulders, winding streams, and rustic bridges, and started up the far slope before reaching the hikers' previous position. The hikers were long gone, and no moose were in the area. As our search continued, three new hikers appeared over a ridge, saw our cameras, and grinned.

"Oh, you guys are going to love this. Just go around three bends, cross a bridge, and you'll see two moose feeding on willows!"

With renewed enthusiasm, we followed their directions, crossing the bridge and scanning the landscape. We were too late. We watched as the mother and calf slipped into dense scrub and vanished. Disappointed, we considered heading back to the hikers' original spot. Maybe some moose had been lying down when we passed earlier? No luck. There still weren't any moose.

As evening fell, the sky darkened with the promise of new snow. It was time to call it a day and hike back up to the car park. With each step, my injured knee

Alaskan moose with little antlers

Alaskan moose approach

throbbed and swelled against the moose-hide splint I was still using after my accident in the Alaska Range. After ascending two-thirds of the way up the slope, I called out.

"Can we stop for a minute? I'd love to record some voice-over footage for my *Wildlife Chronicles* documentary. The valley would be a perfect backdrop." That sounded like a plausible reason to stop and rest. *Wheeze, gasp, wheeze...*

We set up the shot with the far side of the valley as the backdrop and planned what I would say in the voice-over. Snow began to fall in earnest. Nick filmed as I described our misadventure. Suddenly, he stopped filming, threw the phone to me, and grabbed his binoculars.

"You are not going to believe this," he said.

Three moose stood exactly where those hikers had been earlier. They must have been lying down the entire time. Nick turned to me. "We could hike back down, cross the valley, and get to them—or we could go into town and get a burger." I hesitated, weighing further misery against the pleasure of a hot meal and warm bed. But giving up now? No way.

We descended into the valley, made our way around the boulders, crossed the stream, and climbed up the other side toward the moose. Nick talked the entire way about how to behave near mating moose. "Don't stand in their way. If they approach, move aside or back up. The only warning you'll get is a quiet little *huh, huh, huh*. Noted.

At last, we arrived. Two females and a male were engaged in mating behavior. The females grazed calmly nearby, while the bull circled them, occasionally issuing his low warning. When they finished feeding, they settled into tall grass. Only the female's ears and bits of the male's antlers remained visible.

Forty minutes passed, and my knee screamed at me to sit down or walk. Unable to spot the male, I asked Nick if he had moved. "He shouldn't have," Nick said. "But you can check behind those evergreens." I stepped around the trees and froze. I stood face-to-face with a seven-foot-tall Alaskan moose. He sniffed the ground, analyzing the female's scent. He threw his head back, curling his upper lip in the flehmen response—a reaction to detecting the female's pheromones.

Snowflakes spiraled down, settling on his immense frame. He turned and walked toward me just as I started filming. Through my usual 1200mm lens, distant subjects seem deceptively close—but in the heat of the moment, I had forgotten that today, I was working with a much shorter 400mm lens. His antlers filled the frame! Then, I heard it. *huh, huh, huh*. It was very close.

I barely had time to lower the camera before I saw him—a gigantic moose,

Alaskan Moose with flehmen response

plodding straight at me. There was no escaping this. I knew I wouldn't be able to move fast enough to avoid being trampled. As I instinctively turned to run, my injured knee gave out completely, somersaulting me into a bush and out of the moose's direct path. Flat on my back, looking up at the enormous creature retreating into the distance, I realized just how close that had been. It was one of the most exhilarating wildlife encounters in my life.

Nick appeared from behind the trees, casually asking, "How'd the filming go?"

I dusted myself off. "Yeah. It was good. Yeah. Got some good stuff. Yeah."

The hike back felt far less painful. Somehow perseverance, success, and survival had dulled the ache.

Shiras Moose

Grand Teton National Park became our next filming destination. The Tetons are home to pronghorns, elk, grizzly bears, and foxes. But our focus was on finding Shiras moose.

Locals had plenty of advice:

"Just go down to the river."

"Hang out at the trailer park in the morning."

"You'll find them at Moose Flats."

We explored every suggested location, but moose remained stubbornly out of reach. The rule that *wildlife is elusive and can be anywhere except where you are* seemed to be in effect. By evening, with nothing to show for our efforts except a fox sighting, we decided to grab carryout pizza and head back to the cabin.

"I don't care what we see. We aren't stopping for coyotes or foxes," I said. "We are having hot pizza when we get home."

Julie drove through the quiet neighborhood as I balanced the pizza boxes. Suddenly, she slammed the brakes and whispered urgently, "Moose!" There, standing in front of us, was a mother moose with her calf. My plan for hot pizza was immediately forgotten. I tossed the boxes into the back seat and reached for my camera.

"Back up for a better angle," I told Julie.

A male Shiras moose

"I can't," she whispered.

"Why not?"

"The bull moose is right behind us!"

A quick glance in the rear-view mirror confirmed it. An enormous male Shiras moose loomed behind the car. As we sat frozen, he slowly walked around the vehicle, pausing for a moment to observe us.

"Get a picture!" Julie urged.

"I think I'll wait until he moves a bit," I replied, reluctant to capture him with a mailbox reading *The Johnsons* in the frame. Not quite the remote wilderness feel I had in mind. Moments later, the calf began to nurse, the mother grazed on tall forest flowers, and the bull moose posed gracefully among the aspens. When we finally made it home, cold pizza never tasted so good.

Moose Pond

Finding moose quickly became an addiction. I couldn't wait to see more. Word had it that Jenny Lake, a pristine spot where the still morning waters perfectly mirror the Tetons, was a promising location. A ferry carried passengers across the lake to trails leading to waterfalls, so we decided to explore that route, hoping for a sighting. Julie and our daughter Jeni opted for a short hike around the end of the lake, planning to meet my brother and me at the ferry landing.

When we arrived at the landing, the girls were nowhere to be found. Assuming they had started up the waterfall trail, we followed suit. Here's where I should mention that both Brian and I had bad knees, so what was supposed to be a scenic hike quickly deteriorated to a trek more like the Bataan Death March.

An hour passed, and still no Julie, no moose, and no waterfalls. We tried calling, only to find there was no cell reception. Checking our phones on the grueling descent became an excuse to stop every few minutes and try again.

Finally, in one lucky spot, my phone buzzed to life, exploding with messages from Julie and Jeni:

"We never made it to the landing."

"We found moose!"

"Oh, my God! Where are you?"

"You need to get here NOW!"

Attached to every message were cell phone photos. Not one moose. Not two. But FIVE moose.

Female Shiras moose in golden light

I called Julie, who gave us the most crucial directions of our trip: "Take the trail to the left of the ferry and follow it for a mile. There will be a little sign that says—wait for it—Moose Pond."

You have never seen two guys with bad knees move so fast. When we arrived, the moose were still there—two young moose, a large female, and two males. From our vantage point at water level, the filming and photography were spectacular. We watched as a male and female engaged in mating behaviors, while the others stood chest-deep in the pond, dunking their heads and surfacing with dripping aquatic plants clinging to their faces.

Capturing moments of moose emerging from the water, their faces glistening, felt like striking gold.

The Elusive Grizzly

While we primarily searched for moose, there was other wildlife in the Tetons we hoped to capture, including the mighty grizzly bear. It was the right season, and bears should have been out foraging, preparing for winter. Yet, the frustrating truth remained. Wildlife could be anywhere, except where we were.

We continued on our wildlife search, and as we rounded a bend, Julie slammed on the brakes.

"Grizzly!" she hissed.

"Where?" I asked, eyes scanning the roadside.

"You can see his back end—he's feeding in that bush."

Jeni squinted. "Is that the same bush where an elk's head and shoulders are sticking out?"

Julie was firm. "No! It's a grizzly's back end!"

Jeni whispered, "I'm pretty sure that back end belongs to the elk."

"Oh, man! I was sure it was a grizzly!" Julie groaned.

A car pulled up beside us, and the driver rolled down her window. "What are you seeing?" she asked.

Without hesitation, Julie responded, "Some people are saying there's a grizzly in the bushes over there."

Jeni smacked her shoulder. "No one is saying that except you!"

I don't have any photos. It was too embarrassing. We never saw a grizzly.

Elk Whistling and a Cold-Morning Challenge

One of the great autumn spectacles in the Tetons is the elk rut. Bull elk, now sporting massive antlers, battle for dominance and use eerie, high-pitched whistles to claim their territory and attract mates. It would be our challenge to film and record these moments.

Obstacles included:

- Bitter cold mornings.
- Finding the herds in vast landscapes.
- Elk being skittish and elusive.
- Wind, talking, and road noise interfering with audio recording.
- Predawn activity—meaning we had to be in position before sunrise.

After researching, questioning locals, and deciphering conflicting advice, we embarked on our first attempt—driving in the dark through an unlit, twisting road, deep into the high country.

When we reached a high alpine meadow, Julie volunteered to scout ahead, disappearing over a small hill. Minutes later, my phone rang.

"There are elk right in front of me! Right on the forest's edge. Bring the camera—and my gloves. And my hat. And my coat."

I grabbed my tripod, recording device, and excitement, and rushed toward her.

"Shhh," she whispered when I arrived. "They're right there. Do you have my gloves?"

"Umm . . . ahhh, no. I forgot them. Sorry," I stammered.

Julie sighed. At that exact moment, the elk spotted us and bolted into the forest.

What a disaster. At least tomorrow would be another chance.

An Equipment Disaster

Later that afternoon, we turned our attention back to moose. A bridge crossing ahead had all the signs of a big wildlife sighting. There were cars pulled over, people pointing cameras, and the electric buzz of excitement. I opened my door in a hurry, forgetting that my wide-angle lens was on the floor. Unfortunately, the rental car lacked a proper footwell, and the lens tumbled two feet onto the concrete road. The expensive crunch echoed in my soul. It lay there in a dozen pieces. It was beyond repair. We drove home, and I went straight to bed to sulk, but Julie had other ideas.

Ten minutes later, she called me downstairs.

"There's a camera shop in town," she announced. "They have a lens you might like. And they're holding it at the counter!"

We raced into town, found the shop, and purchased a fantastic new lens. On

Bull elk

the way out, I casually asked the owner, "Any recommendations on where to find elk?"

He hesitated. "I'm really not supposed to share local secrets, but since you bought this lens—"

What followed were detailed, cryptic instructions:

- Drive toward Yellowstone an hour before sunrise.
- Pass the beaver pond, then keep going.
- Look for the spot where the big spruce tree used to be.
- Continue 150 feet past the outhouse.
- Turn onto a gravel road, drive a mile, then pull over.

Bull elk breath in back-light

"The elk will come to you."

The next morning, in pitch dark, we followed his directions precisely. As the first light etched the sky, bull elk emerged from the trees, their haunting calls echoing across the meadow. We stood silently outside the car, filming and recording as one magnificent bull wandered closer. I needed to switch to a shorter lens—but my fingers were stiff from the cold. As I fumbled, the camera body and lens separated in midair.

For a brief second, I thought, *This will be fine.* The lens hit the ground with a *thud*, the camera body with a *crunch*. The bull elk raised his head, froze—and bolted. The entire herd vanished into the tree line.

Here is what I have learned about finding wildlife:

- Understand their habits and habitats.
- Remain calm and quiet while in the presence of wildlife.
- Gather good local intel.
- Follow the crowds—if people are stopping, there's usually something worth seeing.
- And, break a lens so you can get reliable info from the camera store owner.

Musk Ox

Musk oxen had always felt like mythical beings to me—creatures of the far north, cloaked in shaggy mystery, dwelling where most mortals dare not tread. They belonged to the realm of storybooks and documentaries, just out of reach and wholly otherworldly.

One afternoon in Tanzania, I shared this lifelong fascination with my friend Nick. His response was instant and classic: "Let's do it!" Within days, he transformed from casual confidant to expedition architect, assembling a travel plan tailored around one goal—finding musk ox in the wilds of Alaska. And in true Nick fashion, he added caribou to the mix, because why not chase every creature that roams the tundra?

Our first goal was to get footage of the great migration of caribou crossing the Kobuk River. One hundred miles north of the Arctic Circle, the Kobuk is on the migration route for hundreds of thousands of caribou. Our Native American guide had a camp on a peninsula overlooking the river

Kobuk River sunrise

where we could stay for days in comfort. However, the caribou didn't care one bit for our comfort, schedule, or film project. They just decided not to show up. For five long days, we waited. Nothing. The migration seemed to have stalled somewhere far beyond our sight. In the end, I left with more photographs of the Kobuk River than I could ever use.

Next, we flew to Nome to meet our guide and friend, Tom Gray, a tribal elder who knew exactly where to position us for filming musk ox. My hope was to capture the behaviors of these Ice Age survivors: head-butting, mating rituals, interactions with calves, and defensive circling.

We ventured deep into the tundra, driving for five hours and covering hundreds of miles before finally spotting a small herd of seven musk ox. The landscape was ablaze with autumn colors, but the animals weren't doing much beyond grazing. Regardless, I made the most of the opportunity, photographing tirelessly until I realized I couldn't feel my fingers. Or my toes. Or my face. Or my ears. In my excitement, I had completely forgotten to put on cold-weather gear. Hobbling back to the car, I stuck my hands in front of the heater, desperate for warmth.

Tom gave me a knowing smile. "It's okay. They'll be here tomorrow. And you'll be ready."

The next morning, we returned, only to find the musk ox had vanished. For an hour, we searched, scanning the tundra.

Nick asked Tom, "Where do you think they went?"

A tundra-ready photographer

Tom shrugged. "It's okay. They're *somewhere.*"

Another hour passed. Then, Tom slowed the vehicle, pulling onto the gravel shoulder.

"I can see them."

We squinted, straining to find the herd.

"Do you see that mountain?" Tom asked.

We nodded.

"Behind it, you can see a saddle with another mountain behind that. They are there."

We stared in disbelief.

"What? That far?"

Tom remained stone-faced. "Yes. There are 27 musk ox up there. You can get to them. Take the trail to the left. The one on the right disappears into tundra and bogs."

I hesitated. "Are you coming with us?"

"No. I know how far it is."

Fair enough. We grabbed our cameras, tripods, and cold-weather gear, and began the trek. The initial climb felt manageable. I was starting to feel the altitude.

Fortunately, Carl, an experienced rock climber, offered advice:

"Rest before you get too tired. Eight deep breaths will restore 80% of your strength."

I nodded. "What about a good nap?"

Nick, who had the stamina of a mountain goat, needed no such advice. After three grueling hours of hiking, climbing, and crossing the saddle, we finally came eye to eye with the herd. The fatigue disappeared instantly. We set up our tripods and cameras, capturing stunning portraits of the musk ox against the tundra's pastel hues. The snow began to fall—thick, drifting flakes transforming the scene into something dreamlike.

The herd wandered over a ridge, and we packed up our gear in preparation for the long journey back. Carl and Nick walked ahead, disappearing around a bend. I followed their voices until I couldn't hear them anymore.

Reaching the saddle, I was confident I could navigate the descent. Gravity helped at first, but soon I was hobbled with fatigue and long past the point where eight deep breaths would help. My water bottle was empty, my thirst relentless. Then, on the final slope, I made a critical mistake. I had strayed onto the boggy tundra path instead of the main trail. I realized my error quickly but had no energy to backtrack. *If I just use my walking poles and tread lightly—*

Wham! My left foot sank into a hidden hole, all the way to my knee. My right leg twisted under me as my camera flew, my tripod hit the ground, and my walking pole snapped in two. Normally, when you take an embarrassing fall, you pop up quickly, brush yourself off, and insist, "I'm fine!" That did

Musk ox in the Alaska Range

not happen in this case. I was stuck, unable to release my right leg. After ten minutes of careful maneuvering, I managed to grab my tripod and use it, along with the broken half of my walking pole, as a support to free my trapped leg.

I knew I was in trouble. I limped the final mile, relying on my tripod as a makeshift crutch. That mile to the car felt like an eternity. When I finally reached it, I collapsed onto the gravel.

Back at camp, Tom's wife cut a piece of moose hide, laced it around my knee, and crafted a splint that I used for the remainder of the trip.

Musk Ox: Day Two

The next morning, my knee was stiff but functional. It seemed good enough for another challenge. Tom had his sights set on a different herd, known as the "Skagway Herd." We drove to a separate part of the Alaska Range, where Tom abruptly stopped the car, pointed at a distant peak, and said, "That's their mountain."

Great. Another mountain. Yes, the herd was there, but with the sun positioned behind them, the light was all wrong for photography and filming. Tom, unfazed, offered a simple solution. "It will be fine. You can hike around the mountain and approach them from the other side." I looked at the towering peak and mentally calculated the effort. *What have I gotten*

Musk ox herd in the Alaska Range

myself into? Not wanting to be "that guy," I forced enthusiasm and shouted, "Let's go!"

Tom drove as close as possible to the mountain base before dropping us off. With cameras, tripods, and backpacks strapped in place, we started our ascent, angling ourselves for the best possible light behind the herd. Nick, ever the fearless guide, assessed the landscape. "If we climb over this ridge, we should end up behind them with a perfect shooting angle." That all sounded good. Until, at the ridge's peak, I lifted my head and found myself face-to-face with an 800-pound musk ox.

I let out an *AAHHHRG!*

The musk ox let out an *AAHHHRG!*

I fell backward. He bolted toward a small valley. So much for a slow, subtle approach. But at least we were close to the herd now.

We couldn't have asked for a more stunning scene—thirty-four musk ox scattered across the valley and mountainside, framed by the vast expanse of the Alaska Range. Mothers tended to their calves, males charged at one another, and an enormous bull commanded the herd.

We filmed tirelessly, capturing every movement, until the bull suddenly gathered his group. As if responding to an unseen signal, the entire herd lay down, heads tucked low. Confused, I turned to look behind me.

That's when I saw the dark storm clouds, heavy with snow, racing toward us. The blizzard struck and I yanked on my warmest coat, hat, snow pants, and gloves. With nothing else to do, I found shelter behind a boulder, used my backpack as a pillow, and let exhaustion take over. I woke an hour later, dusted off the snow, and, unbelievably, had my camera ready just as the

Musk ox preparing for a storm

musk ox began stirring. When they shook off layers of fresh snow, their thick, shaggy coats created an incredible display. The slow-motion footage turned out to be utterly breathtaking.

Bighorn Sheep on Wild Horse Island

As winter deepened and the far north became inaccessible, Nick, Carl, and I turned our focus south, to Montana and its dramatic bighorn sheep. Nick lives near Flathead Lake, 27 miles long, encompassing nearly 200 square miles, and containing a dozen small islands, the largest being Wild Horse Island, featuring peaks rising 3,000 feet above the lake. A place of legend and wildlife, Wild Horse is celebrated for its wild horses, bighorn sheep, and, as we'd soon discover, mountain lions.

The three of us glided across the lake in Nick's 20-foot motorboat to a sheltered cove on the island's leeward side. As we unloaded tripods and camera gear, Nick laid down the rules:

- Stick with me unless I'm scouting.
- If I'm scouting, stay put.
- The rams are in rut, so don't get too close.

With water bottles and cameras in hand, we set off. I had yet to see a doctor about the knee I injured in the Alaskan Range and was forced to take it slow. Carl, ever patient, matched my pace while Nick bounded ahead like a mountain goat.

We hiked through pine forests, over soft ridges and valleys, past an ancient apple orchard frequented by browsing horses, and into open meadows. Rounding a sharp bend, we found Nick crouched beside the remains of a bighorn kill. Despite official claims that mountain lions don't inhabit the island, the tracks told a different story. Nick scanned the area and urged us to stay close. My knee felt deceptively fine, so I pressed on.

We combed the lower reaches of the island, checking all the usual bighorn habitats with no luck. Nick suspected the mountain lion's presence had disrupted their routine. Eventually, we spotted a herd of 21 sheep: mostly ewes and four sub-adult males.

"These aren't the sheep you're looking for," Nick said, channeling his inner Obi-Wan.

Bighorn sheep

"Stay here; photograph them as they head to the water. I'll scout for the rams. Stick together!"

We filmed for over an hour before Nick returned.

"I found them," he said. "But you're not going to like it. Look up at the last ledge near the summit. We don't have to go, but if you're game, it'll be worth it."

It felt like Alaska all over again. The choice: climb 3,000 feet or risk being taken by a mountain lion. Self-preservation won. What looked like a 45-minute hike turned into a 90-minute grind—one foot forward for every foot of elevation. But the payoff was spectacular.

We found a powerful herd: nine mature rams and a dozen ewes. The males were posturing with horns touching, bellies kicked—a prelude to full-on jousting as they challenged each other. We also captured stunning portraits of rams with record-breaking horns.

The sun dipped behind the mountain, and it was time to descend. Downhill proved harder on my knee than the climb, though mercifully faster. We retraced our steps, passing the site of the lion kill. Nick froze mid-step, finger to lips. A massive male mountain lion padded across the path and vanished behind a boulder. Every hair on my neck stood up—we were not the apex predators here.

Bighorn sheep butting heads

We moved cautiously toward the cove. Nick, pressed for time, went ahead to prep the boat so he could navigate the lake before an approaching windstorm hit. Carl and I agreed to follow the path. Nick disappeared over a ridge, and we followed—only to realize half an hour later that nothing looked familiar.

In my best Gandalf voice, I said, "I have no memory of this place."

Carl replied, "Don't look at me. There are four genes for sense of direction, and I'm missing three."

Brilliant outdoorsman that I am, I said, "We're on an island. How hard can it be? Okay. If we follow the shoreline, we'll find the boat." We kept going until we found the shoreline, but twilight had fallen, and a sign revealed we were three coves down and eight miles from our destination.

Unfortunately, the trees descended straight to the water with no

Bighorn sheep portrait

footpath. All we could do was keep the lake in sight. Then darkness fell. Carl kept a steady pace while I dropped farther behind with my stiff and swollen knee. I couldn't see Carl ahead of me. Rustles in the surrounding forest were surely a lion stalking us. Everyone knows they go for the slow and weak one, right?

When we finally reached the cove,

Nick was gone. He had left the boat and some bottled water and gone searching for us. We spotted his cell phone light when he returned. It seems we'd missed one crucial turn, just over the ridge where he had left us.

The lake was black as oil under a moonless sky. With no lights at the ramp and navigating by cell phone glow, we somehow found the right spot to land. I would never have believed it possible that I would feel this depleted twice in one month.

BRAZIL'S PANTANAL

There are some animals that, despite their power and allure, I may never photograph. Bears, for example. Bald eagles, for another. Traveling solely to capture a single species has never been my approach. I prefer destinations that offer a complete ecosystem, where apex predators thrive alongside a diverse cast of supporting species. Brazil is one of those places.

The Pantanal, the world's largest tropical wetland, is home to giant anteaters, Brazilian tapirs and vibrant scarlet macaws. Abandoned cattle ranches, once devastated by drought, have been reclaimed by nature and transformed into eco-lodges where wildlife flourishes. At one of these restored farms, it's easy to hike along quiet trails and photograph kingfishers snatching up small piranhas, or to drift through waterways filming hawks, jacanas, or even swarms of sulfur butterflies on riverside mineral licks.

Here, jaguars dominate the waterways, moving silently through dense vegetation. But they are not alone. The same areas hold pumas, giant otters, ocelots, and hundreds of species of birds, making every outing an unpredictable encounter with nature at its wildest.

Jaguar sightings in this region are unmatched—each trip yields an average of nine to fifteen unique individuals. Remarkably, over the years, at least fourteen of these majestic cats have been newcomers, either passing through or settling into the area. One of the most electrifying moments is witnessing a jaguar silently stalk and ambush a Pantanal caiman, one of its preferred prey. Just as captivating are encounters involving multiple jaguars,

Mating jaguars

whether it's a mother with her cubs, a clash over territory, or the graceful dance of courtship.

Alone in a Boat

We were warned that a female jaguar had been seen roaming the grounds of our eco-lodge. In another season, two jaguars were observed in mating behavior. On a boat excursion, we unexpectedly spotted them across the river. Surreal. Stunning.

On this trip, though, no jaguars had been reported on the grounds. They must have moved on to a new territory. Instead, we had a rare avian species to film, the great potoo. The potoo is almost impossible to detect. It chooses its perch meticulously, blending into tree bark so perfectly that even experienced naturalists can walk right past one without noticing.

We navigated the river to a landing near where a potoo had been seen. As we disembarked and began the trek, I noticed that Sue, a member of our group, was missing. Heading back, I found her still in the boat.

"I'm just tired," she said. "I'm not really interested in the potoo. I'll stay here and rest until you guys get back."

I hurried to catch up with the group and was just in time. They had found a pair of potoos. The female sat on a gray branch that perfectly matched her feather pattern. The multi-colored male was perched on a tree trunk that matched his hues. Not only that, but a tiny chick poked its head out from under the female's breast! It felt exciting to be able to photograph these difficult-to-find birds! The return trek had turned into a boisterous reliving of the event when our guide suddenly halted, his attention focused on the ground.

"Jaguar," he said, pointing at fresh tracks in the mud. The atmosphere shifted. The leisurely walk through the woods became something else entirely. We all felt a frisson of danger, bunched closer to the guide, and started looking around with every step. Sue would regret missing this.

Jaguars on the river bank

When we reached the boat, something felt off. Sue sat frozen in the back of the boat, her eyes wide.

"What's wrong? Are you okay?"

She barely managed to speak. "T-t-two j-j-jaguars just c-c-came down the path an-an-and put their paws on the s-side of the b-b-boat! Th-they left when you g-g-guys got b-b-back!"

That must have been terrifying!

Heading home, we spotted what we thought were three giant otters swimming across the river.

"Those aren't otters," the boatman said. "Those are jaguars."

We followed them as they emerged from the water, coats dripping with every stride. Their path led them within 100 yards of our cabins. It was the kind of experience that lingers, leaving us forever changed by the wild natural history we've witnessed.

FLAMINGOS

Flamingos are an iconic, global species native to tropical and subtropical regions, with six known types. Chilean, Andean, and James's flamingos are native to South America. American (or Caribbean) flamingos are found in South America, Central America, Florida, and the Caribbean islands. And the most widespread and numerous are the greater and lesser flamingos, mostly distributed throughout Africa.

They are all vibrantly colored, with plumage ranging from pastel to flaming crimson. When they gather in numbers, their behaviors are riveting, from flight take-offs and landings to group mating dances and rhythmic feeding. The best photographic angle is always at eye level.

The size of a flamingo group depends on water levels, chemistry, and food supply. They prefer to congregate at hot springs that have blue-green algae, crustaceans, and aquatic invertebrates. The richer the nutrients in their diet, the greater the saturation of pink in their feathers.

Of the six species, the smallest is the lesser flamingo, on average half the size of the greater flamingo. Their beaks have evolved and adapted to their diet. Lesser flamingos have a deep-keeled bill, more deeply curved and trough-like for filtering algae and tiny organisms from the water. In contrast, the greater and American flamingos are up to 60 inches high. Both have thicker, shallow-keeled bills, which allow them to filter feed and eat seeds, insects, and small fish.

Both the alkaline lagoons of Turks and Caicos and the soda lakes of East Africa's Great Rift Valley are ideal flamingo habitats—abundant in algae, insects, and mollusks, and ideal for courting, nesting, and raising chicks. My next adventures would take me to these places to film the supermodels of the bird world.

Caribbean Flamingos

While making the documentary *Avian Chronicles*, I knew flamingos had to be included. Their vivid color, distinctive behavior, and range of habitats made them an obvious choice. With six species in the world, I had already filmed four, leaving the American flamingo next on my list.

After research and advice from seasoned travelers, we decided the Turks and Caicos would be the ideal filming location. We packed the camera gear, sunscreen, and snorkeling equipment—planning ahead for scenes in another documentary, *Oceans*—and flew to the islands to settle in.

Our villa was breathtaking and stocked with everything we could need, including a fruit basket and a fine bottle of rum. It felt like the perfect home base. My brother Brian immediately claimed the title of Pool Boy and Bartender, keeping the rum punch flowing as we recovered from a long travel day.

A detailed map of the islands outlined the best flamingo-watching spots, and we wasted no time. Flamingo Pond, Flamingo Meadows, Flamingo Creek. Unfortunately, each destination turned up empty.

Going further afield, we tried Flamingo Lagoon and found thousands, but they were impossibly far away. That left us blindly searching for other options. One involved a ferry ride to a series of islands connected by bridges and causeways. We explored until the final stretch of road led to nothing but open ocean. Every likely habitat was deserted. It felt like time to call it quits.

Julie suggested a picnic, and the map pointed us toward a quiet north shore beach. We followed a road leading through a tunnel of Australian pine trees. As we neared the beach, something spectacular happened. Through the tunnel, we could see the golden sand, the striking blue Caribbean water—and streaks of vivid pink dropping from the sky. Flamingos were raining into the ocean.

Caribbean flamingos

"Go! Go! Go! For the love of God, GO!" I shouted—calmly, of course.

Julie skidded to a stop at the tree line. We had arrived.

In the rush to get my camera, I fumbled with my seat belt. I was trapped. I couldn't get it open. Panicked but exhilarated, I finally freed myself and could take in the scene.

About twenty-five Caribbean flamingos had landed in shallow waters formed by sandbars. Their older chicks had been brought here to stretch their wings and practice flying. Again and again, the adults ran across the clear shallows, taking to the air with their young trailing behind. They circled the lagoon, returning to the same sandbanks for landing drills.

I captured shot after shot, but on a quick review, I found that none of them did justice to what I was seeing. In my excitement, I had overlooked the best angle from which to photograph. That angle existed only where the beach met the waves. Dropping to a sitting position in the sand, I could finally frame my shots correctly. These were some of the most dramatic flamingo images I had taken since Lake Nakuru.

When the young birds had finally learned their lesson—or perhaps when the tide changed—the flock made a final take off and disappeared over the horizon. Only then did I realize we had the beach entirely to ourselves, except for one old islander who had watched with us. He introduced himself as Leonard.

"Did you enjoy da show?" he asked.

"Yes!" we said. "Does this happen often?"

He shook his head.

"No. I've been comin' to dis beach for sixty-five years, and I've never seen anyt'ing like dat."

From that day forward, we call this stretch of sand "Leonard's Beach."

Flamingos on Lake Nakuru

The famous real estate saying is *Location. Location. Location.* In many ways, wildlife photography follows the same principle. If you want to photograph tigers, go to India's Kanha National Park. If you want to film wildebeest crossing the Mara River, go to Kenya. If you want great photos of giraffes, visit Lake Manyara. And if you want to see millions of flamingos, your

Flamingos on Lake Nakuru

destination should be Lake Nakuru.

Lake Nakuru, one of the many lakes formed by the Great Rift Valley, is home to lions, giraffes, buffalo, an impressive population of white rhinos, and famously, leopards. While the park is too small to support elephants, the wide, shallow, brackish lake provides the perfect habitat for brine shrimp and krill, the preferred food source for both greater and lesser flamingos.

Depending on seasonal rains, water depth, and soda content, all of which influence food availability, Lake Nakuru can host up to 1.5 million flamingos at a time. The sheer number of birds alone can offer stunning scenes, but there's more to capturing the moment than simply photographing a sea of feathers. Their feeding behaviors, interactions, and aerial movements, whether flying solo, in squadrons, or in vast formations, make for exhilarating photography.

One fascinating aspect of the flamingo story at Nakuru is predation. African fish eagles and tawny eagles prey on flamingos, while marabou storks scavenge along the shoreline. Interestingly, the eagles' normally yellow beak lores take on a distinct pink hue from their flamingo-heavy diet.

One of the most intense spectacles occurs when packs of hyenas charge into the shallows, scattering flocks of feeding flamingos in search of injured birds to prey upon. The first time I witnessed this, we raced along the lake shore, paralleling the hunt and photographing at full speed.

Photographers were also allowed to exit their vehicles and shoot from the lake shore itself. The lower angle made for striking images of incoming flight and landings. Lying flat on the ground allowed for an ethereal view, separating the flamingos from the foreground and

Zebras that caught my attention

background in a dream-like way.

When this technique is paired with their elaborate mating dance, in which anywhere from nine to one hundred males dramatically circle a female, vying for her attention, the result can be riveting.

On an August morning, three of us were shooting from a spot right at the lake shore. One photographer stood, another sat on a box from our vehicle, and I was lying flat on the ground—if you can call flamingo poop "ground"—with soft light illuminating the flocks. The effect was breathtaking. Shot after shot captured the elegant birds as they fed, sparred, and stretched their wings. Then, something unexpected happened. Three zebras thundered past behind us, kicking and nipping at each other. The other two photographers weren't interested. The zebras weren't birds.

I was fascinated by their behavior, but by the time I twisted around in the flamingo muck, I had missed the moment. However, in missing it, I gained something far better. The zebras disappeared, revealing eight male flamingos performing a mesmerizing courtship dance around a single female.

I was in the perfect position, thanks to the zebras, and fired off twenty vertical shots. That moment became the pinnacle of my photographic flamingo career.

BBC Wildlife Photographer of the Year Competition

When I returned home, Julie fell in love with the series of photos, and we selected one to enter in the BBC Wildlife Photographer of the Year competition. It won the Bird Behavior category, and they flew us to London for the awards ceremony, held at the Natural History Museum. When we arrived, I realized I hadn't packed a dress shirt.

"No problem," Julie said. "We'll just go to Harrods."

I had been to London many times but had never stepped inside Harrods. I knew it was expensive, but the store exceeded all expectations. The cheapest white button-down shirt cost just over 500 pounds. But you know the old saying. *In for a penny, in for 500 pounds.* At least I looked good at the awards ceremony.

The host presenter, a British TV personality, had the audience engaged from the start. When the flamingo photo went up on the big screen, he said, "I know what you're thinking. There have been

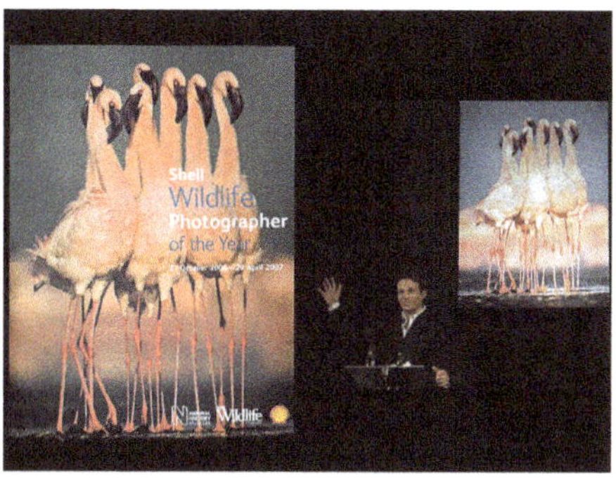

BBC Wildlife Photographer of the Year ceremony at London's Natural History Museum

more flamingo photos entered in this competition than there are flamingos at Lake Nakuru. But—just look at it!"

Banners featuring the flamingo image were spread all over London, announcing the exhibit. When the exhibition went on a worldwide tour, I had friends call from Germany, France, and Australia, saying they were standing in front of my flamingo photo. When the tour stopped at Yale University, I was able to bring my children and my parents to see it.

All thanks to three zebras and a lot of flamingo poop.

INDIA

India is an ancient land of mystery. Lost temples, misty jungles, and the Taj Mahal are legendary. Its wildlife is fascinating and diverse. Wild elephants, one-horned rhinos, antelope, and colorful birds all offer a photographic challenge, but the king of them all is the Bengal tiger.

When I first started photographing Indian wildlife, there were only 1,400 tigers in the wild, with more being in private zoos in Texas. However, I have worked with Amit Sankala, whose grandfather is responsible for Project Tiger, without which we would not have *any* tigers. Amit's influence has helped expand parks and enlarge buffer zones in order to give tigers more space. These efforts, coupled with increased tourism, have resulted in tiger numbers ballooning to over 3,500 tigers in the wild.

I used to love leopards. They were my favorite cat. Then I saw a jaguar. They became my favorite. Then I saw my first tiger. Nothing can compare to the power, texture, beauty, color, and grace of a full-grown tiger.

Whenever we would arrive at Amit's tiger lodges, I couldn't sleep with the excitement and uncertainty of what the next day would bring. Now, I sleep like a baby lion because I know his guides and trackers will inevitably find tigers for us. The mystery is when, where, and what the tiger will be doing when we find it.

A Memorable Sighting

It was Julie's and my first visit to India with our dear friend and guide, Harendra. We had been out several days, and we had not yet seen a tiger. Harendra told us how to look for fresh tracks, how to read the weather, and how to know which tigers lived in what areas.

Harendra also taught us the importance of alarm calls and how to be in tune with the sounds of the forest. Spotted deer, sambar, and barasingha deer all have different vocalizations when they see a tiger. Langur monkeys have keen eyes and treetop vantage points. Their alarm calls are very reliable. On this particular drive, we heard the monkeys, but they were coupled with a crucial element—the calls were moving, which meant the tiger was

Our first tiger

moving. The edge to Harendra's voice was unmistakable.

"Get ready! He's coming."

Nothing could have prepared us for the next moments. Harendra jumped up in the jeep and yelled, "Tiger, tiger, tiger!"

On cue, the tiger strode into the clearing, looked at us, and rumbled a deep-throated growl that we felt in our bones. He seemed to say, "Beware. I am the tiger!"

It took a couple of hours for our hearts to stop pounding. Nothing else seemed to matter. We didn't care what else we saw. We had seen a tiger.

Moments later, Julie asked, "Do you think we'll see another one?"

The Elephant, a Bush, and the Tigers

Elephants play an essential role as both guardians of the tigers and in maintaining the equilibrium of the vast tiger reserves. Riding high on their backs, mahouts have an unparalleled vantage point, enabling them to monitor shifting territories, detect signs of new cubs, observe conflicts, and deter poachers. Their knowledge of the jungle is encyclopedic. One sweltering afternoon, Harry turned to me and said, "We've got a chance to ride an elephant today. They know where the tiger is. Plus, I've got a brand-new camera. This will be a perfect time to test it."

A mahout rode high atop a stately bull elephant as it strode toward us

Bengal tigers

across the savannah, stopping just beside our Gypsy vehicle. Using the jeep as a makeshift ladder, we hoisted ourselves up onto the mahout's platform. It felt like we were climbing onto the roof of a house—thrilling and a little nerve-wracking. But Harry's excited chatter about his camera kept our spirits light.

The mahout guided our elephant through dense forests, shallow streams, and wide grasslands until we reached a thick patch of shade beneath a tree. The mahout pointed and quietly said, "Tiger."

And sure enough, deep in the undergrowth, we could just make out the faint shimmer of stripes. But I wasn't there to just spot a tiger. I came to photograph one. I gently voiced my wish to the mahout. Without missing a beat and accompanied by the quiet pressure of his feet, he softly commanded, "Hut, hut. Hut, hut."

With stunning precision, the elephant took two steps forward, wrapped its trunk around the underbrush, and swept it aside using trunk and foot in perfect coordination. And there they were—not one, but two breathtaking Bengal tigers, lounging in the shade like kings.

In his excitement, Harry lunged for his camera and accidentally sent the lens cap spinning off the platform, landing squarely between the two tigers. His face crumpled in panic. "My new camera!" he groaned.

The mahout didn't flinch. "Hut, hut, hut. Hut, hut, hut."

The elephant extended its trunk, reached delicately between the two tigers, lifted the lens cap with remarkable grace, and handed it back to Harry. Honestly, it was one of the most impressive things I'd ever seen.

ORANGUTANS IN BORNEO

Borneo was where I finally hit my limit. The relentless heat and physical strain of photographing in the jungle pushed my torn meniscus past its breaking point. Walking became unbearable. After a grueling hike in 110-degree heat and 100% humidity, I was finally able to put my knee up and tried to cool down in my 99-degree room. That's when our guide pounded

Orangutan

on the door, yelling, "We found an orangutan with a baby—just up the hill!"

"Just up the hill" turned out to be a steep, three-quarter-mile climb. I grabbed my big lens and macro, because you never know, and started the trek. I could see my group ahead, pointing excitedly into the towering rainforest canopy. But by the time I arrived, the moment had passed. The mother had whisked her baby into the treetops and out of sight.

Deflated, I turned and began the slow walk back to the lodge. I was nearly there when one of my clients called out, "Hey! There's a stunning red, white, and black butterfly—just bring your macro!" Grateful to ditch the heavy lens, I set it on the ground and hiked 100 yards back uphill and found it: a six-inch marvel, wings spread like stained glass.

I had just started photographing when a voice came from further up the hill. "She's moving! The orangutans are low. You can see the baby!"

I sighed. *Of course you can.* I trudged downhill to get the big lens, then climbed the full three-quarters of a mile again. And, naturally, by the time I got there, the mom and baby were gone.

The descent was brutal. I could no longer bend my knee. Sweat sprayed from my hair and clothes with each lurching step. I collapsed on a fence post, unable to stagger the last fifty feet to my room. Julie brought me a liter of water and supported me the rest of the way. I was drenched, dizzy, and exhausted. I decided the best strategy for drying off was to walk straight into a running shower, fully clothed.

CREEPY CRAWLIES

Tiger Leeches

Borneo's steamy jungles teem with wildlife begging to be photographed—Asiatic elephants, orangutans, hornbills, slow lorises, and jungle cats weave a dramatic tapestry of life. But it's the reptiles and invertebrates that fill in the finer details: crocodiles and monitor lizards patrol the waterways, while snakes and insects haunt the dense forest undergrowth.

All these exotic subjects were on my photo checklist. But one species not on the list lurked in the back of my mind—the tiger leech. These bloodthirsty predators can latch onto your shoe, rapidly scale your leg, and jump from foliage onto your arm or head. And here's the best trivia note on tiger leeches. The Latin name is *Haemadipsa picta*— meaning painted bloodthirsty one.

I tried not to dwell on it, but in researching the best leech defense, I found leech socks—thigh-high socks designed to prevent the little vampires from crawling to places you'd rather not imagine. I advised all the clients to pack a pair.

We then reached Danum Valley, rumored to be crawling with tiger leeches. Sean, one of our team members, joked, "Ten bucks says we never unpack those leech socks." I should've taken that bet.

Our first jungle outing was a macro photographer's dream. We found ornate mantises in every color, furry bats roosting in rolled-up leaves, and lizards and snakes galore. We continued our trek, first along a boardwalk, then a dirt trail, and finally into a small glade beside the river.

"There are no leeches in this jungle," Sean declared.

Noted.

We were all chasing insects

Tiger leech

with our macro lenses when Karen, another team member, called out, "Hey, what do you think this is?" She pointed to a chubby, orange-striped worm on a leaf. She crouched closer for a better angle. Then, in a scene straight out of *Alien*, she screamed and jumped backward when the "worm" elongated to three inches, reared up, and vaulted towards her face.

Someone shouted, "TIGER LEECH!" and all hell broke loose.

Where moments before there had been only foliage, now every leaf and stem held a tiger leech—hundreds of them—their bodies stretching and swaying toward anyone who drew close. In gleeful abandon, we spread out, each finding a bush for leech photography. At first, the silence was only interrupted by exclamations about how beautiful the leeches were and how best to photograph their unique behaviors, then later, by faint cries for help to remove them from our hands, legs, necks, eyes, and even under some shirts as photographers' bloodless bodies slumped to the ground in their last moments of life. This tale may be slightly over the top, but everyone needed a leech check before we started our hike back to the lodge.

At lunch, Sean announced he wanted to try photographing the leeches in mid-air as they propelled themselves at us. He also made it clear he'd be wearing his leech socks or possibly a leech hazmat suit.

After revisiting what we now call "Tiger Leech Grotto," every single one of us had been bitten. One member marched to the hotel manager's desk, hands on hips, and declared, "I was bitten by a tiger leech!" The manager smiled, reached under the counter, and with a flourish, handed him a certificate. "You are now a member of the Danum Valley Blood Donors Society."

A Rare Find

That night, a jungle hike was scheduled, but I felt so drained that Julie suggested we skip it. We settled into the open-air lounge with cold drinks, letting the jungle sounds wash over us. We wished good luck to Cindy and Jeanne, the two sisters on the trip, and leaned back to relax.

We were halfway through our second drink when Cindy burst into the lounge, barely able to speak. When she caught her breath, she said, "Todd! You've gotta come. Now! I know you're tired, but trust me. Grab your camera and flashlight!"

Leaf-legged katydid

She led us back down the jungle boardwalk to the infamous Tiger Leech Grotto. "I hope he's still here," she whispered, sweeping her flashlight across the foliage. "There he is."

I squinted. "All I see is a bunch of leaves."

"He *is* the leaves," she hissed.

And there it was—perched at eye level on the end of a branch—the most astonishing insect I've seen in sixty years. Its body was a perfect mimic of a leaf. Its front legs looked like leaves. Its back legs were shaped like two sets of leaves. I filmed and photographed it from every angle.

Back at the lounge, Jeanne was waiting with a Cheshire Cat grin. When a preeminent entomologist like Jeanne says something's important, I listen. She explained that this leaf-legged katydid was one of the most significant insect discoveries of the last decade when it was reported in 2016.

"We only found it because I recognized its distinctive chirp," Jeanne said. "At that point, I knew exactly what I was looking for."

A Master of Disguise

One of the finest naturalist guides I've ever known is my dear friend, Yehudi Hernandez. Based in Costa Rica, Yehudi spends his days exploring the jungles and cloud forests in search of the rare and dramatic species found in Central America. I've learned a lifetime of natural history from him during our treks for species, ranging from the elusive Honduran white bats, which ironically don't live in Honduras, to countless species of hummingbirds, to dazzling resplendent quetzals.

He's the one who showed me the subtle but profound differences between two-toed and three-toed sloths. And no, it's not just the number of toes—they're entirely different species, each having evolved similar traits and behaviors to thrive in the same environment. Together, we've photographed more species than I can count.

But one discovery stands out above all the rest.

We were walking through a jungle glade when Yehudi suddenly raised his hand, motioned me over, and pointed to a slender leafy branch. Hanging from it was what looked like a small brown viper. I'd never seen anything like it.

Then he did something that made my heart stop. He extended his finger toward the creature's mouth. The snake began to sway, moving into its strike posture. I instinctively pushed his hand away, fearing the worst.

*Moth larva mimicking
a viper*

He just smiled, gently parted the surrounding leaves, and revealed the truth. It wasn't a snake at all. It was a larva, a caterpillar on its way to making a cocoon, which in turn emerges as a moth. Its shape, color, texture, and movement had evolved to mimic a venomous viper. The illusion was so convincing that most birds would steer clear, mistaking it for a real predator.

Years later, I learned that my friend Jeanne Shirley, a very enthusiastic entomologist, had helped describe this exact species as new to science back in the 1970s.

Dung Beetles

With over 7,000 known species in Africa, dung beetles are found on every continent except Antarctica. These industrious insects thrive in a wide range of habitats—farmlands, forests, grasslands, prairies, and deserts—but they're especially drawn to places rich in animal waste, particularly from herbivores. That makes the Serengeti Plains a paradise for these remarkable scarab beetles.

Dung beetles play a vital role in ecosystems. The most important is clean-up duty, getting rid of tons of excrement that would otherwise overwhelm the Serengeti. They roll small dung balls for food and to attract mates. Large, orange-sized "brood balls" are buried deep underground to nourish their eggs. In addition to cycling nutrients, improving soil structure, and promoting growth of foliage, the dung balls disperse seeds. Undigested

Dung beetle rolling dung

seeds—like those from an elephant's foraging—can be transported up to a mile when a beetle rolls its dung ball away from the source. Their tunnels also boost the soil's ability to absorb and retain water, enhancing overall fertility.

Another astonishing thing about dung beetles is that they navigate using celestial cues, such as the Milky Way or polarized light from the sun. Periodically, they spin on top of the ball in a navigational dance to reorient themselves. They then balance on the ground with their front legs and push the ball with their hind ones, impossibly but rapidly reversing the brood ball in an unswerving line.

A goal of our expedition to the Serengeti was to film the behavior of beetles. With the great migration of wildebeest and zebras sweeping across the plains, there was no shortage of dung. All we needed was open ground, plenty of beetles, and—ideally—no lions.

We found the perfect spot and set up for breakfast. The drivers arranged tables, chairs, and picnic baskets right on the open plains. When the coffee was ready, they called us to eat—but no one was listening. Everyone lay belly-down in the grass, photographing dung beetles. I had to use a cattle prod (figuratively, of course) to herd them into the breakfast line. We grabbed a quick bite and got back to work.

Every behavior was captured: beetles selecting fresh droppings, rolling their chosen bits, solo rollers, duos working in tandem, and the burial of completed larval nests. It was a textbook shoot.

After packing up and driving fifteen miles, someone suddenly said, "I lost my phone at the breakfast spot."

Salvatory said he could find it. Out of the entire, vast expanse of the Serengeti, he amazingly drove straight to the spot.

Everyone left the vehicles to look for the phone, fanning out from the jeeps. Thirty minutes later, no phone, but we found even more dung beetles. We all asked if it would be okay to start shooting again. While we were occupied, Salvatory climbed into the client's Land Cruiser and immediately found the phone tucked deep in a seat pocket. We were given another ten minutes with the dung beetles before we headed out again.

HATCHING SEA TURTLES

There is really nothing like watching sea turtles hatch on a deserted tropical beach.

In nesting season, sea turtles return to the beaches where they were born and lay several nests of eggs, with over 100 eggs per nest. The incubation period is approximately sixty days, meaning we can then anticipate when the eggs will hatch and when to be there to witness and photograph one of nature's dramatic life moments.

The hatchlings in each nest dig to the surface and emerge at the same time. They sense where the ocean is and race in that direction, moving surprisingly fast for turtles. Their strong flippers propel them across 100 meters of sand, rocks, driftwood, and vegetation to the water's edge, where the tide then sweeps them into the ocean.

They have to move fast. The mortality rate for green sea turtle hatchlings is as high as only one in 10,000 surviving to adulthood. Their first challenge is to make it off the beach to the water. They need to outrun dogs, foxes, crabs, hawks, and

Baby sea turtle—100mm macro lens

Baby sea turtle entering the ocean—15mm fisheye lens

vultures. Our guide informed us that an unexpected benefit to allowing select photographers near the nests is that it protects the babies from predators.

I have filmed over fifty sea turtle hatchings, and each one is unique. They tend to emerge in the afternoon when the sand is warm and the tide is receding. The beach around the nests can be smooth, rough, clean, or crowded with obstacles. The choice of lens will determine what kind of pictures you will get. Long lenses and macros isolate the hatchlings, while a wide-angle lens allows close-ups of the turtles and includes the entire beach scene.

My favorite turtle photography is done with a wide-angle lens mounted to one of my inventions, the "Turtle-Cam 2000." This setup can be smoothly operated four inches away from a racing turtle.

Now for the story. On a deserted beach, I was filming hatching green sea turtles as they raced to the ocean. One of my favorite shots is the exact moment when the hatchling is carried into the ocean by a receding wave. It's tricky to do because the wide-angle lens needs to be close to the turtle and the water, meaning the camera equipment can be swamped at any moment.

I concentrated on staying close, giving the baby turtle space, and not getting soaked, when I heard distressed shouting.

"You are too close to the turtles! Stay away from the turtles! Move away! Get away!"

I looked up to see two red-faced birdwatchers on the beach waving their arms and yelling at me. I was all alone as my guide had walked further up the beach.

I stopped filming and walked over to the lady who had been yelling at me. I smiled, introduced myself, then chatted about how my biologist guide and I had been coming to this beach for 20 years to film endangered sea turtles for documentaries. I shared with her my own concerns about endangered wildlife and explained how my filming technique would not impede a turtle from entering the ocean. In fact, our very presence creates a safe environment because predatory birds won't take them if we are here.

The lady wasn't having it. After enduring more fury and finger-wagging from her, I walked twenty meters away and sat on a driftwood log. The beach was now cleared of humans. Three seconds later, a mangrove black hawk swooped down, grabbed a baby sea turtle, and flew off.

Watching the bird of prey vanish into the clouds, I was again struck by the fragility of our world and how conservation is a delicate balance between active safeguards and simply providing undeveloped space for animals.

And I'll never forget the silhouette of the hawk gripping the hatchling in its talons as it flew into the setting sun.

KAUAI AND THE COURTSHIP DANCE OF THE ALBATROSS

The island of Kauai is a serene gem of tropical wilderness, a haven for seabirds, marine life, and relaxed photography. Julie and I visited Kauai on several occasions and filmed Laysan albatross in different stages of life. As filming for the documentary *Avian Chronicles* neared completion, we realized we were missing a critical piece of the Laysan albatross story—the theatrical courtship rituals that seal their lifelong bonds.

After fledging, Laysan albatross embark on epic solo journeys, gliding on trade winds for up to five years without touching land. Eventually, they return to breed where they were hatched. Adult pairs return to the nesting sites every year and rejoin to raise a single chick. It's an annual ritual, and we were determined to capture it.

Julie, ever the research wizard, pinpointed a remote site with minimal human noise, perfect for video and audio work. The challenge? It was New Year's Eve, peak tourist season, and the only available access was through a private estate that allowed albatross viewing combined with tours of the

Mother Laysan albatross and chick

grounds. Our only option was the "Garden and Statuary" excursion.

Our guide was sincere and gracious. We politely smiled at New Age sculptures and learned exhaustive floral biology during our promenade, all the while biting our tongues and biding our time. When the last of the "garden people" had shuffled off, the guide quietly ushered us to a locked gate.

Beyond the gate was a hidden world—a forested cliff packed with active albatross nests. Birds bobbed and bowed in greeting, clacked beaks like castanets, and generally raised joyful cacophony. I wandered onto the peninsula to scout landings while Julie slipped into the woods with her gear. Our guide kept a watchful eye on us. When she realized exactly what we were trying to accomplish, she began her albatross check list of mates, nests, and eggs.

Minutes later, Julie called out, "Hey, I'm getting great behavior. Look at this greeting!" Two albatross were deep in a synchronized dance. A chain-link fence marred the backdrop, but the ritual was mesmerizing. Then came the fateful line. "My headphones are acting up.

Older Laysan albatross chick

They're just hissing."

I assumed it was a loose cable in her headphones. Our time ran out, and the guide was waiting for us, telling us we had to go. Before we left, I showed her some of the amazing footage we took. She drove us to the gate and waved goodbye. "Happy New Year," she said, handing us her card.

The Audio Fiasco

Back at the hotel, we reviewed the footage. Visually? Stunning. Audio? A persistent hiss, devoid of bird calls. The culprit? A barely visible *ON/OFF* switch on the mic switched to *Off*. Classic.

"No problem," I said optimistically. "We'll just go back tomorrow and—Nooooo!" Slapping my forehead, I realized what I was saying. The next day was New Year's Day. Everything on the island would be closed, including the Garden and Statuary Tour!

Julie didn't flinch. "Let's call the guide and see if there's any chance of getting back in."

I was already composing a desperate, groveling pitch when she answered on the first ring.

"Sure," she said, island calm in her voice. "I'll be checking nests anyway. Meet me at 9:00."

When It All Came Together

The next morning felt like a gift. The colony buzzed with activity. Albatross soared in from sea, reuniting after a year apart. Julie found a female nesting in clear view—no fence, no distractions. I filmed a male's comical landing and his wobbly entry to the nesting site. He headed straight to the female Julie had been filming.

Then magic.

The pair began the greeting ritual—beak clacking, high-stepping, spinning, braying like donkeys, celebrating their reunion with unfiltered joy. Audio? Crisp. Video? Gorgeous. Behavior?

Laysan albatross head-bobbing greeting

Laysan albatross beak clacking greeting

National Geographic!

When a BBC crew saw the footage, their jaws dropped. "It would've taken us three months to get anything that good," they said.

Maybe. Or maybe they just needed Julie, a hidden forest, and a New Year's miracle.

THE OCEAN REALM

The fourth installment of the *To the Ends of the Earth* series, titled *Oceans*, draws deep inspiration from my father, who was a zoologist. On many of our family holidays, he took us to the Indian Ocean coast, to places like Kigombe, Ras Kazone, Pangani, and Tanga Beach, which became our open-air classroom. It was there, ankle-deep in tidal pools, that Dad taught us about the creatures of the sea. I've written more about those formative lessons in the second section of this book.

Julie shares that love of the shoreline. Over the course of ten years, our holidays as a married couple revolved around exploring fragile marine habitats and sea life. We journeyed through the Gulf of Mexico to the Caribbean Islands—Grand Cayman to Barbados, St. Lucia, Aruba, Turks and Caicos—and along the East African coasts of Kenya and Tanzania, as well as the South Pacific's Fiji and Cook Islands, and even to Australia's

Great Barrier Reef. Later years brought us to the Maldives and several islands in Hawaii.

A Shifting Tide

Our first filming expedition for *Oceans* was to Turks and Caicos, where local intel directed us to a rocky section of beach that fronted three vacation homes. We were told to keep an eye on those homes as a landmark (I now understand the meaning of that expression) because the tide turned quickly there and it was easy to get swept out to sea. *How bad could it be if we simply pay attention to the tides?*

Batteries charged on the Super GoPro, and with snorkels and masks secure, we began our underwater adventure. I was concerned when the water was not as clear as I expected. Visibility dropped, and the reef seemed lifeless. I filmed out of sheer habit, poking my head around coral heads and into crevices, searching for marine life. When I finally spotted a promising sponge formation and kicked toward it, I couldn't make headway. Julie had vanished from view. I tried reaching for a coral outcrop, but I was still five inches shy, and no matter how hard I kicked, I could get no closer. I was in trouble. The tide had shifted, fast and unforgiving.

I recalled a survival tip. Let the current carry you, then swim parallel to the shoreline. It worked, for the most part—we reached the beach safely, but nearly a mile down the shoreline. Our hearts raced, but our bodies and souls were intact.

After waiting two hours for the neap tide, we returned to our access beach. The transformation was astonishing. Calm, crystal-clear water greeted us. Patches of sand sparkled between rippling beds of eel grass. While filming ocean floor textures, a sea turtle emerged from the grasses.

I'd never seen one in the wild. This hawksbill was breathtaking, its amber shell catching the sun. Instead of diving down twenty feet to film him, I hovered at the surface, knowing

Our first hawksbill sea turtle

he'd have to come up for air. With a glance and a stream of bubbles, he tilted his head as if inviting me to witness the secrets of that aquatic wonderland.

That footage—quiet, clear, and intimate—gave me the confidence to chase stories through the world's tropical seas and bring *Oceans* to life.

The Maldives Islands

Few ocean creatures have captivated me like the whale shark. Despite their imposing name, these gentle giants are neither whales nor apex predators. They are massive, slow-moving filter feeders that migrate across all tropical oceans. Out of their many habitats, the 1,200-island Maldive archipelago would be our staging ground to find them.

Julie spearheaded the research, zeroing in on an island atoll that offered three essentials: prime snorkeling reefs, proximity to feeding grounds, and a price tag that wouldn't sink our budget. By then, I'd upgraded to using an Ikelite underwater housing, custom-built for the same mirrorless camera I used for on-land wildlife photography.

Getting there was no small feat. We flew from Chicago to Paris, Paris to Qatar, then to Malé, and finally took a seaplane to the remote atoll. Our resort was sublime. It was elegant, efficient, and the perfect launchpad for our underwater expedition.

To reach the whale sharks, our dive captain provided a 100-foot schooner for an overnight sail to their feeding grounds. It happened to be Julie's birthday, so the crew set a candlelit dinner on deck as the sun melted into

Whale shark, Indian Ocean

the horizon. After dessert and music, we retired to our teak-paneled suite and drifted off to the gentle rhythm of ocean waves.

By morning, anticipation crackled in the air. I scanned every small whitecap and shadow in the water, imagining each could be a whale shark. But as the hours passed, I couldn't shake the mantra: *Whale*

Whale shark, Indian Ocean

sharks can be anywhere—except where we are. Other boats then began arriving. Our early lead vanished. Now, I dreaded that we'd find a shark only to be crushed in an aquatic flash mob.

Sure enough, a distant boat stopped and several dozen snorkelers plunged into the water. I asked our captain if we should follow. With a seasoned smile, he said, "By the time we get there, he'll be long gone."

Just as our hopes began to fade, the whale spotters began pointing and yelling, "Shark! Shark! Shark!"

As instructed, we donned masks, snorkels, and fins, then elegantly toppled off the boat. As the bubbles cleared, we found ourselves staring right at a forty-foot whale shark, gliding effortlessly through the blue.

I wasn't ready. Not for the size. Not for the grace. And certainly not for what followed in his wake—a horde of twenty-four frenzied snorkelers,

Whale shark, Maldives Islands

thrashing, kicking, and churning the water as they tried to keep pace with the fish. Some were guides trying to photograph their clients near the whale shark. Others had selfie sticks that they were using as clubs.

The next thing I knew, someone kicked the mask off my face. My snorkel flooded and my lungs filled with water. I had to let my Ikelite camera housing float while I gasped and choked, trying to readjust everything.

Meanwhile, the underwater roller derby mob swam by, still chasing the whale shark but far behind him now.

And then, chaos met choreography. Julie swims like a fish, and she pulled ahead of them with her underwater camera. The thrashing mob had no idea what they were up against. Her footage was gold with head-on shots and gliding profiles—everything we hoped for.

As the worst swimmer in the ocean that day, I resorted to my strengths: stillness and luck. Then—shouts from the deck of, "Don't move! He's coming to you!"

Sure enough, in the blue haze, I spotted him. He headed straight for me. I powered on my camera, wiped the bubbles off the dome port, and held my breath. I'd planned to stay still and hope he would come to me. Somehow, miraculously, it worked. The leviathan grew larger with every beat of his tail. It took several minutes for the behemoth to pass beneath me before he dove into darkness.

The footage was a triumph. But what I remember most is the final swish of that massive tail—passing inches from my mask—a farewell brush from one of nature's most glorious creatures.

Reef Manta Rays

The Maldives are renowned for their reef manta rays. Once whale shark filming was a wrap, we turned our attention to these graceful giants. While not as massive as giant mantas, their oceangoing cousins, reef mantas can still span a formidable twelve feet from wing tip to wing tip.

The locals knew where the cleaning stations were and timed our outing for low tide, which favored our chances. We showed up at the dock loaded down with cameras, underwater housings, towels, sunscreen, and plenty of water.

Our speedboat shot past half a dozen atolls to the site where mantas had been spotted the day before. Nothing. We moved to a second promising reef. Still nothing. By the third site, my subconscious was playing a familiar loop: *Rays can be anywhere—except where we are.* It seemed appropriate. We eventually returned, disappointed. The resort staff greeted us, looking genuinely heartbroken on our behalf.

At breakfast the next morning, they were beaming. "The boats went out before dawn. They found the rays!" Julie, ever the realist, opted to sit this one out, convinced her absence would guarantee a sighting. Dr. Hunt was game. We grabbed our gear and rushed to the boat.

This time, we motored beyond the usual chain of islets into open ocean. When we hit deeper water, we found them—eight reef mantas no longer lingering at the cleaning station but engaged in a "mating train" formation. It's a mating ritual of slow, synchronized figure eights as males follow a female in graceful pursuit.

It was visually mesmerizing but challenging to capture. We hovered forty feet above them, far deeper than my preferred three-to-eight feet for easy duck diving. I shot some footage. Not only was there too much water between me and the rays, but the wide-angle lens made the mantas seem distant and diminished.

Then came the internal dialogue: *I have to do it. Should I do it? Could I do it? No. Yes!*

Before I could change my mind, I took five rapid breaths and one deep inhale, and dove, kicking as hard as I could, straight to the ocean floor to meet the mantas eye to eye. The film footage captured the synchronized, avian-like flapping of their fins as they glided through the courtship dance. I filmed until I realized I'd forgotten to take still images. Typical. But I was out of breath. I began my ascent, aware of the distance and aware of the

Reef mantas and a trumpet player

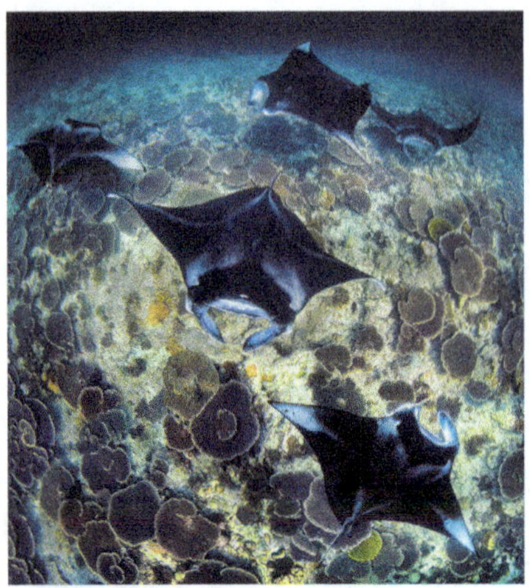

Reef mantas in a "mating train"

growing urgency in my lungs. I started re-breathing, unsure how much farther I had to go. Then—breakthrough. Surface. Air. Relief.

Floating there, watching the mantas continue their hypnotic ballet, my brain offered the obvious: *I have to do it again. Should I? Could I? No. Yes!* Once more unto the breach. I dove again, this time promising myself I wouldn't stay down as long. Since I make my living using my lungs to play the trumpet and my breath-holding record is four minutes, I knew I could get the pictures I needed and still make it back to the surface in safety.

This time down, I noticed the rays were executing their figure eight patterns over colorful table corals. As the group had broken up into two separate circles, I moved over to the group that was dancing over the most dramatic and colorful corals. The photos were a success, and the fact that I am able to write this chapter is evidence that I survived the ascent.

Stingrays in Grand Cayman

Returning to the western hemisphere, we knew exactly where to go to film and photograph southern stingrays. Though they're found throughout the Gulf of Mexico and tropical seas, the ones in Grand Cayman's North Sound are in a league of their own. They are larger, bolder, and conditioned to seek food from fishermen cleaning their catch.

These stingrays live on the shallow, sandy flats of the North Sound, where clear turquoise water makes them easy to find.

We'd vacationed here and visited the rays before, so we were familiar with the challenges. But this was our first serious attempt at capturing footage for the *Oceans* documentary, and that raised the stakes. Cruise ships were our nemesis. Not only did they release hundreds of tourists into the shallows—ankles and legs bobbing into the frame—but they also churned

Giant stingray and sea grass

up the sand and ruined the water clarity. Julie found a private boat captain who understood everything we needed. We left at dawn, beating the crowds to the sandbanks by hours. Along the way, the captain familiarized us with stingray behavior and biology. One new regulation for us was no fins or flippers in the water. Fine by me. It would mean less sand kicked up, resulting in clearer shots.

The sandbanks were alabaster white, set against the vibrant blue of the Caribbean shallows. As we dropped anchor, shadowy round shapes glided in our direction. The rays had arrived.

I slipped into the knee-deep water and was instantly engulfed in a vortex of stingrays. From the deck, Julie filmed me in the eye of the storm, stingrays swirling all around. Too many, in fact, to film clearly. I floated away from the boat, letting the crowd thin. No food on me meant fewer rays, and soon there were just a handful gliding around me, framed perfectly for the lens. Silver jacks trailed beneath their bellies, gleaming in the filtered light.

As the days went on, a few truths about filming in the shallows crystallized:

- Even underwater, light angle is everything
- Water clarity can make or break a shot
- Choppy seas scatter shadows and reflections in distracting ways
- Gently undulating water casts a dreamlike mosaic on the seafloor
- A calm, mirror-smooth surface delivers the most even, ethereal lighting

The final footage showed stingrays swooping in elegant unison, barring jacks stealing food in lightning assaults and eel-grass rippling against the white seafloor. The tapestry of life in the world's oceans was starting to take shape.

Mafia Island

Mafia Island has become a true home away from home and one of my favorite destinations on earth. Its marine national park is a sanctuary of untouched coral reefs, swirling clouds of tropical fish, live seashells, towering coral pillars, moray eels, sea turtles, and vast fields of anemones brimming with clown fish. Every low tide reveals a chance to snorkel in this living aquarium.

Each outing here hinges on timing. One hour before the turn of a neap or new tide can offer up to four precious hours of filming. Photography choices often boil down to which lens to carry. A macro lens lets you get up close and intimate with a subject, while a wide-angle keeps you near your subject but lets the surrounding habitat breathe into the frame.

As with all photography, light matters. Angle, intensity, and softness all play a role. But, as another underwater challenge, water quality enters the mix. The best days are glassy, windless, and timed with the middle of a tide cycle. The worst? When wind, wave, and tide stir up sand, or when nature throws in a twist.

The ocean that day started as calm as a lake. But as we neared the reef, dark storm clouds built above us, and soon rain began to fall. No wind. No lightning. Just a steady downpour. We figured it wouldn't matter. We'd be underwater, after all. What harm could rain do?

We entered the shallows near the reef, hoping to film anemones and clown fish. I brought the camera to my eye, and everything was warped. I blinked, thinking something was in my eyes. Maybe the problem was in my mask. I rinsed it, but the view was still wavy, unfocused, hazy. I dove for a closer look, and suddenly everything clicked into sharp focus. Back at the surface? Blurred again.

What felt like a vision problem turned out to be physics. The cold freshwater from the downpour had formed a viscous layer atop the warmer

Wide angle photo of clown fish on a pristine reef

saltwater, distorting the view like a lens smeared with Vaseline. It would take hours for that layer to dissolve. Our filming day was done.

But the ride home was its own reward: steel-gray storm clouds towering over a glass-flat ocean, the sky reflecting in every direction like a three-dimensional watercolor.

Coconut Crabs – Chole Island

Mafia is more than just a single island. It's a nine-island archipelago, each with its own specialty.

Mafia has the coral reefs. Juani is known for its sea turtle nesting grounds. And Chole? It's home to crabs. Lots of them. Among the most spectacular is the coconut crab, a palm-sized hermit in youth that sheds its shell and grows into a three-foot-wide behemoth.

Though found across the Indo-Pacific, coconut crabs are elusive. They avoid the sun and only emerge after dark, which makes sightings rare and fleeting. But word was Chole Island had them. So, we chartered a twilight journey, needing a high tide to reach the island and arrive as the crabs became active.

The ocean was a mirror as we neared Chole, dusk painting the mangroves bronze. We searched for a gap in the mangroves that would lead us to where the crabs would appear. The gap turned out to be a narrow inlet of shallow water that was only negotiable via a sketchy-looking dugout canoe.

I was asked to get out of the main boat and climb aboard an absurdly small dugout that was about 15 inches across and 4 feet long. *Absolutely not. Not happening*, I thought. I may even have said out loud, "No way, man! No way in hell!" Then the boatman calmly took my hand, and against all laws of physics, helped me get one foot into that tiny wooden vessel. He held the dugout steady while I flailed my arms and desperately grabbed mangrove branches, trying to get my other leg in and sit at the same time. I tumbled into the canoe with all the grace of a falling wardrobe.

Just for reference: I'm 6'6" and 230 pounds. That boat rode low. We're talking half an inch of clearance before it became a bathtub.

Still, somehow, we made it to a quiet lagoon surrounded by a beach of crushed coral. It was stunning. The boatman went back for Dr. Hunt, and while he paddled away, I lay back, stared at the fading sunset, and watched

Coconut crab

the Milky Way rise in a velvet sky, black as ink.

Soon, we had cameras and flashlights ready. As it became fully dark, a parade of crabs emerged from the surrounding mangroves. The first crab was yellow, the next blue, then pink. The last to appear was a brilliant plum-colored specimen. Each species sported vivid hues, as if someone had spilled an artist's paint palette into the mangroves.

Then came shouts and the rustling of bushes. The guys had found a coconut crab. A monster burst from the underbrush and scuttled across the coral beach, its massive claws with a vivid blue and red pattern and a thick, coiled tail under its body. But instead of walking, it launched itself backward with that tail, flinging itself toward the lagoon like some sort of Olympic crustacean athlete.

We scrambled to intercept and redirect it up the beach, just long enough to grab our footage. Then we let it continue on its evening quest for fruit and conquest.

Of course, we still had the return journey to consider, only this time in reverse, at low tide, and now in darkness. Flashlights helped us pick our way back to the main boat.

The crescent moon had set. Above us shone the spectacular Milky Way, and all around us stretched black, glassy water.

That's when I saw it—not just above, but below us. The Milky Way's shimmer was mirrored by marine bioluminescence stirred by our passing. The boat slipped through a glowing ribbon of light, stars above and stars below. And, as if in a dream, we cruised straight through the middle of it all.

Manatees

Manatees are similar to whales and dolphins, in that they are mammals who adapted to a life entirely in the world's oceans. Along the Gulf of Mexico, manatees winter in the sheltered embrace of tranquil estuaries. These gentle giants—once mistaken for mermaids by weary sailors—gather by the hundreds in freshwater springs, drawn to the warmer temperature. They've been on my wildlife species list for decades, and at last, the chance to see and film them became a reality.

Julie and I did our homework. We searched for the clearest waters, lowest crowds, and the right temperature range to ensure a prime window for filming. We found a local boat captain who swore he could get us to the right spot at the right time for peak manatee density and minimal human traffic. We booked two days for the shoot, just to be safe.

The first morning, the Crystal River greeted us with a brisk chill. By the time we suited up at the dock, it was full-on freezing. The boat's deck was wrapped in plastic sheeting to block the wind—a good sign for manatees, not so much for us. The captain assured us these were ideal conditions. When it's cold, the manatees huddle in the warm estuary waters. He gave us the rules:

- No touching manatees
- Stay at least five feet away
- Don't block or crowd them

Easy enough—until it wasn't.

When we arrived at the lagoon, the sun had just started to rise. The water, shaded by ancient live oaks, looked like liquid obsidian. Slipping into the spring was shocking, but not in the way I expected. Compared to the air, it felt warm and inviting. I cleared bubbles from the camera dome and began to search. Visibility was almost nonexistent.

Then—*thump*. Something enormous nudged my left side. I turned to see a shadowy figure the size of a school bus pressing against my shoulder. Remembering the five-foot rule, I instinctively tried to move, only to get gently bumped a second time. I was now sandwiched between two mammoth manatees. I saw no sign of Julie. It was just me, trapped and thinking, *This would be such a strange way to die.*

Trying to remain calm, I figured I'd just duck under them and swim free, until a third giant glided beneath me, brushing my stomach. *Will I get in trouble for being so close? I'm touching manatees! I'll never get out of this! It's not my fault! These guys are way too close to film. Hey, it's nice and warm here. Could I get crushed? I think I'll hang out here till they decide to leave.* They

Manatees in the warm waters of an estuary

eventually drifted off, granting me my freedom. As the morning progressed, light filled the lagoon, illuminating a dream-like scene. There were manatees everywhere, drifting, spiraling, barrel-rolling. I captured stunning footage, but what came next was pure magic.

I spotted shafts of spiraling light rays cutting through the dark. As I filmed, something stirred in the deep. A massive form began to rise, slow and surreal. Out of the gloom swam a lone manatee, perfectly framed in the golden beams. *Don't panic! Don't panic!* It approached, stared directly into the lens, then turned and vanished into the gloom, leaving only ripples and chills down my spine.

That moment alone was worth every shiver, but the ride back was brutal. I am sure we teetered on the brink of hypothermia. The wet suits offered no warmth, and changing into dry clothes on deck felt like cruel punishment. We shivered so hard we could barely hold the cups of hot cocoa the captain offered. Most of it ended up on the deck. It didn't help that the pontoon boat ride back was over forty-five minutes in 20-degree weather.

My arms trembled, and my numb hands couldn't grasp buttons or zippers when I tried to get dressed. I thought I'd have

Manatees floating in the Crystal River

to just wrap myself in a blanket, except there wasn't one. *Next time, bring Himalaya gear*, I thought. *Who knew you'd need it in Florida?* I tried to tell Julie, but it came out, "Wumma mumma morida."

Once home, we threw down our gear, headed straight to the hot shower, then passed out under a mountain of quilts. When we finally stirred, our first task was to call the boat captain and cancel the next day's trip. We'd gotten what we came for—and more.

PART THREE

East African Mission,
Childhood in Tanzania

My earliest memories and my personal journey to the ends of the earth began when I was only two years old. My dad was approached at a church potluck by a representative of the Lutheran Church of America about plans to build a school in a place called Tanganyika. His background in education and science, plus his skills as a machinist, were perfect for the job. He was forty years old with a teaching career and three children. And he said, "Yes!"

Three months later, the house was packed, including Mom's upright piano, and we had tickets to fly to Tanganyika by way of Athens. It's easy to remember events from my early childhood. To me, things happened either before or after we moved to Tanganyika. Athens was before. I can remember sightseeing, going from site to site on a small touring bus. It was hot chasing my older brother, Brian around the Acropolis. Back on the bus, the taste of a cold soda from the cooler was unforgettable.

A Broken Collarbone

The main event in Athens occurred when we were leaving the Plaka Hotel for the airport. Mom and Dad checked out at the desk while I chased my sister Jane around the hotel's entryway. I somehow lost my balance, careened into a stone pillar, and fell so hard I couldn't get up. I felt pain like never before in my short life. A stranger found me on the sidewalk and carried me to my parents. I can still hear Mom's voice as if it were yesterday, saying, "You've broken your collarbone."

Indeed, I had, and it would cause us to miss our BOAC flight to Nairobi. The doctor set the bone by wrapping my shoulder, chest, and back in a cast. He said I looked like Tarzan and would be right at home in the African jungle. It was around that time that we discovered our flight had been canceled. One of the engines needed to be replaced. I guess all's well that ends well.

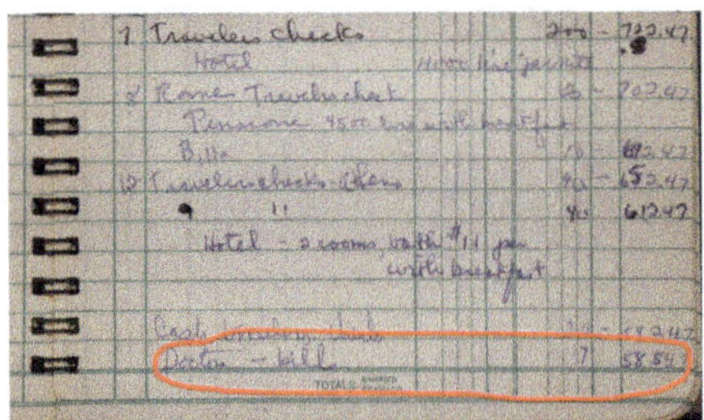

Mom's ledger even included the hospital's fee for setting my broken bone

Life in Tanganyika

But it hadn't ended yet. We still had to get from Nairobi to Tanga (a port at the foot of the Usambara Mountains), and the only aircraft Dad could book was an old DC-3. The interior was slanted so steeply that I remember telling Mom it was like climbing a hill. We had the first five seats, with our luggage right behind us, and the rest of the plane filled with crates of squawking, newly hatched chicks.

From Tanga we transferred to Magamba and stayed in teachers' homes

Our DC3 plane

until our belongings arrived and got sorted out. Brian was to attend the English school just down the mountain in the German hill town of Lushoto. When Mom and Dad visited the school to find out about the start of the semester, school supplies, and such, they were told in no uncertain terms that Brian wasn't qualified to attend. He hadn't taken the two years of Greek and three years of Latin required of all students. One of the American teachers at Magamba Secondary School told Mom about a mission school called Kiomboi, located 500 miles away. The bus that was chartered to transport the northern district students was leaving from Moshi in two days' time. With no other options, we packed the car and drove the 170 miles to spend the night in Moshi's KNCU Hotel. Having just arrived in Tanganyika a few days before, we had jet lag. It caused us to oversleep the morning we were to meet the bus. When we rushed to the bus stop, we were told it had departed hours before. Without hesitation, Dad bought some food for a picnic lunch, filled the gas tank, and proceeded to chase down the bus to Kiomboi!

The roads in Tanganyika at that time were not what they are today. The 45 miles between Moshi and Arusha took most of the day, and we didn't catch the bus until about 30 miles past Arusha when it stopped to allow the kids a bathroom break. Children ran around the bus and into the bush.

Brian said, "I think it's them."

Jane, Mom, Brian, and Todd having one of Mom's famous picnics on the road

The Safari Hotel

Once Mom and Dad had Brian's school situation taken care of, and since our belongings had not yet arrived in the Usambaras, we took this time to drive to Arusha and move into the Safari Hotel.

Anyone who has been on a Tanzanian safari has passed through Arusha and driven by the antiquated Safari Hotel. When we moved there in 1961, it was shiny and new. It became our home for three months while Mom and Dad attended language school to learn Swahili. I celebrated my third birthday in that hotel's restaurant. My gifts were a book about a toy duck, called *Flannel Feet*, and a pegboard with colorful wooden pegs for creating patterns and pictures. My granddaughters now have both toys.

While we lived there, the movie *Hatari* was filmed. John Wayne led a star-studded cast playing adventurers traveling through East Africa working for the Berlin Zoo. What I remember is Dad taking me for a haircut and making a big deal about a guy in the next chair. It was John Wayne. There's a scene in the movie with a famous music score behind it called "The Baby Elephant Walk" by Henry Mancini. In the scene, one of the three baby elephants goes crashing through Singh's grocery store. Every time I watch the movie, I wait for that scene. It's the store where we did our weekly shopping.

THE USAMBARA MOUNTAINS AND MAGAMBA

The Usambara Mountains are 7,000-foot rainforest-covered mountains located in the northeast corner of Tanzania, situated about halfway between Mount Kilimanjaro to the west and Tanga on the coast. After language school, we moved back to the Usambaras outside the small village of Magamba.

The barrels with our belongings had arrived, and we had a "house" to

Magamba Village

live in—Flint Cottage. It was a pair of round huts connected by a great room, beautifully constructed with hinged doors and windows with glass panes. Local *fundis* (craftsmen) had made floor-to-ceiling custom, curved sh elves in the round hut areas. Jane and I

Mom in front of Flint Cottage

had one hut for a bedroom, and Mom and Dad the other. I suppose the windows and doors could have been a little tighter. On two occasions, we were invaded. Once by frogs. The tiny amphibians had hatched in the marsh, and we stood in their path to their new forest habitat. The entire floor of the house became a moving, hopping, jumping mass of little frogs. The second invasion happened when a massive battalion of *siafu* (army ants) came in right under the door, marched across the floor, up the wall, and out the bedroom window. My skin still crawls when I think of it.

Jane and I played "school" with Mom outside of the back door while Raphael, our housekeeper, cooked dinner. Flint Cottage was built on a sloping hill that descended to a reed-filled marsh said to be inhabited by green mambas. The only way to get to the school was for Dad to make the long trek around. Out of respect for Dad, the students built a 100-meter-long bridge above the reeds. I

The headmaster's house

*Jane, Todd, Mom, and
our new puppy*

was terrified to cross it. In my mind, if you strayed near the edge of the walkway, you would be instantly bitten by a green mamba.

We stayed in Flint Cottage for almost a year. Michael Chesterman was the headmaster of Magamba Secondary School. He and his wife Sylvia lived on the other side of the valley with their three sons. In the ebb and flow of post-colonial Africa, Michael caught the attention of someone high in the Church's structure who had influence and didn't like Michael's political views. He was given a week to pack his family and belongings and leave Tanganyika. Through a vote among the northeast teachers and missionaries, Dad was chosen as the next headmaster of the school.

We moved from Flint Cottage to the headmaster's house, which was quite upscale from Flint Cottage. It had running water, electricity, tight doors and windows, separate bedrooms for each of us, and a kitchen.

*Usambara dwarf
chameleon*

I spent my days holding fast to Mom's skirt when she walked from the new house through the forest to the school. The lush, tropical environment was home to chameleons, silky colobus monkeys, and clouds of butterflies that filled the air on sunny days

Our backyard was the mountainside, which included our vegetable garden and raspberry patch, while the front held flower beds and a badminton court constructed by Dad. We reconnoitered the jungle, ran through the gardens, and terrorized the cook and gardener.

*Usambara colobus
monkey*

Jane and the Billy Goats

One day, two billy goats appeared in the raspberry patch on the mountainside above our house. They belonged to the chief of the village just over the ridge. Richardi the gardener wasn't around, so Mom gave Jane a long stick and told her to move the goats out of there. Jane, who was all of six years old, bravely marched up the slope with that stick.

One of Jane's goats with Richardi

She yelled, "You goats! You get out of here!"

Both goats turned to her, put their heads down, and charged! All I remember seeing from behind Mom's skirt was Jane flying headlong down the mountain, followed by two deranged goats. She ran full speed through the open kitchen door and into the house, followed closely by the goats. She made a sharp right turn into the living room, while the goats turned left into the laundry room. They stayed trapped there until the chief of the village came and paid a ransom of three chickens.

Magamba Secondary School

Dad was now the headmaster, working the equivalent of three full-time jobs as a teacher, administrator, and head of the school building project. He could only do this with Mom's help. Mom and I made a daily trek through the Usambara Forest to bring him lunch. We showed support for the school's extracurricular activities like boxing matches and basketball games by standing courtside for every event.

School-aged boys from all over East Africa came to Magamba Secondary for their education. It was cold at 7,000 feet in the Usambaras, and many of the students came from much warmer

Magamba Secondary School

Class photo of Magamba students

areas of equatorial Africa. The British boarding school model required a uniform of pressed, short-sleeved white shirts and dark shorts. Students would line up every morning for inspection. It was mandatory at these early morning inspections to check the cleanliness of the dormitories and the school dress code.

The long and short of it was, the boys were freezing. Although initially dismayed at how the system failed the boys, Mom promptly worked on a solution. She ordered yarn and knitting needles, then held knitting classes for the students. Those handcrafted hats and sweaters made all the difference in their comfort and health. To this day, there are fathers in the Usambaras who teach their sons how to knit warm clothes.

One of Mom's piano students

That's not all Mom did to open new doors for Magamba students. She taught piano on the upright she had shipped from the States. She had lots of fine students over the years who took quarterly exams sent to Magamba from the London Royal Academy of Music.

Tanga and the Indian Ocean

Down the mountains and 60 kilometers away sat the bustling Port of Tanga, where exportation of sisal helped finance a post office, a hospital, banks, and the Twiga Hotel with its rooftop restaurant. I loved visiting Tanga when I was little. At the toy store, I would breathlessly gaze through the glass-topped counter at things I could only

Todd, Jane, and Laurie Lindell in Tanga

Family and friends on Kigombe Beach

wish for, like a cowboy hat, a cap gun, and coloring books.

In Tanga, we always stayed with the Lindells, a missionary family who ran a church in the Tanga district. We visited them for Christmas, and imagine my joy when I received a cowboy hat, a cap gun, and a coloring book. However, I did have a problem when I thought Mom said to "stay in the lions" when I colored.

Brian, Jane, and Todd on Kigombe Beach

While visiting Tanga, we would often drive down the coast to Kigombe Beach. That was where Dad taught me about tropical sea life. Together we explored the tidal reefs, turning over rocks, digging in the sand, and examining seashells in the tide pools. He showed me the different shapes of shells and how the animals moved and lived. This experience sparked my future fascination with marine life and inspired my love of nature.

ON SAFARI

To celebrate my cousin Priscilla's graduation, she and my grandmother visited us for a safari.

In the 1960s, safaris were heroic undertakings. Not only were the roads

Newspaper clipping from Pricilla's safari

rough, but they petered out to nothing in some areas, making driving at night impossible. And if that weren't bad enough, rhinos were known to attack vehicles in the dark. Our Austin wasn't built for rugged safari travel, but this was family, and Gustafsons never shied away from adventure.

As we slowly and carefully maneuvered through the mountain forest, we startled a Cape buffalo. These enormous animals, weighing up to 2,000 pounds and sporting curved horns a meter across, are notoriously aggressive. They are ranked among the top five most dangerous animals in Africa.

This one crashed up the mountain in a panic to get away, only to careen down the slippery underbrush and slam into the side of our car. He landed eye to eye with Grandma. It was hard to know who was more terrified. Apparently it was the buffalo, who freed himself and scrambled away.

Dad and an expert mechanic with our trusty Austin in various states of disrepair

Lake Manyara

Our first game drive was in Lake Manyara National Park. This was before there were any proper roads. Instead, they had tracks, and we were allowed to drive off-road through the grass and mud and go cross country.

The park was a wonderland of animals with thousands of Thomson's and Grant's gazelles, impalas, and zebras. Herds filled the meadows near the lake. When Dad drove toward them, gazelles leapt and sprinted in all directions, flying through the air. It was the most beautiful thing I had ever seen.

"Do it again!" I cried.

Dad went for it, hit a bump, came down in an aardvark hole, and broke the Austin's axle.

The guards at the front gate knew we hadn't checked out. As afternoon faded to evening, it seemed no one was coming to find us. When full darkness fell, we could see from the flickering lights in the distance that they must have been searching on the other side of the park.

We sheltered in the car and watched sunset color the sky with every shade of red, orange, blue, and purple. We had premium, front row seats at the side of the lake. Giraffes glided along on their impossibly long legs, silhouetted against the sunset's glow. Elephants trumpeted past, our car shuddering with every footfall.

The inside of the car was unbearably hot and stuffy, but we couldn't lower the windows because of mosquitoes. When it started to rain, Mom desperately held out a Coke bottle to catch a few drops, but all she seemed to catch through the open window were more mosquitoes.

In the morning, Dad decided to walk out to get help. He must have had the luck of the innocent. He passed countless elephants, lions who had just eaten, hippos, and a crocodile sleeping in a pool. He returned hours later in a jeep with other safari folk. They promptly offered us a canteen of water. I've never tasted anything so delicious.

Ngorongoro Crater

The next stop was the one and only Ngorongoro Crater. Mom had told me all about it. It was a giant crater, shaped like a bowl, and there were animals

Dad photographing the Crater from the same spot 25 years later

in there—lots of animals. When we stopped at the Crater overlook, I was too small to make out anything over the tall grass. Dad picked me up and helped me stand on a boulder so I could see. To say I was underwhelmed would be an understatement. As a four-year-old child, I expected giant animals vaguely resembling Animal Crackers crashing around in a cereal-bowl-shaped crater. From 1,000 feet up, I couldn't see a thing!

Fast-forward 25 years. When my wife Julie and I took Mom and Dad back to Tanzania to visit Magamba Secondary School, we stopped at the same Crater overlook. Dad was now in his seventies and couldn't find a spot where he could see. I thought, *I know where there's a boulder that will help!* I hoisted Dad onto the same rock he used when I was three years old and supported him the same way he had held me.

Now that they've "upgraded" the overlook and installed a concrete viewing platform with guard rails, I don't stop there anymore.

BOARDING SCHOOL

Kiomboi was a school for missionary kids. Students from all over Tanzania attended for 10 weeks on, two weeks off. Mom and Dad drove 800 kilometers through rural Tanzania to get us there.

When I entered the first grade, I joined my brother and sister at the

Kiomboi missionary school. I well remember those long drives to and from Kiomboi. On those marathon trips, it seemed we were always stopping for flat tires, washed-out bridges, or animals on the road. My favorite trips were in a borrowed VW bus that had a fold-down table and chairs that we'd set up by the roadside when we needed a break. I played

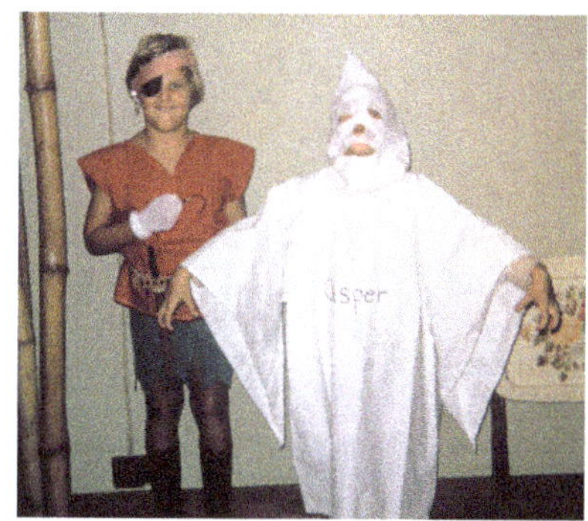

Halloween at Kiomboi

games at the table, and snacked on delicious Moshi bananas.

At the school, Fred and Martha Malloy were in charge. We lived in dorm rooms and underwent inspection every day. This is where I learned rules about having clean fingernails and making tight hospital corners on the bed. I also, unhappily, learned about demerits and how having too many would ruin my free time and chance for desserts.

When I was in first grade, Jane was in second, and Brian in eighth. As an eighth-grader, Brian was one of the kings of the boarding school. The "big kids" were responsible for the *shamba* (garden) and also for activities like putting on shows, leading sporting events, and directing games. Brian embraced the role fully then and continued to do so as an adult, when he became a teacher, singer, and accomplished community theater actor.

During one memorable Halloween, we all dressed in costumes. I was Casper the friendly ghost, while Jane, who loved the *Peter Pan* books, dressed as a pirate. Although everyone said I looked cool, I couldn't see a thing through the costume's eye holes. I was really Casper the blind ghost.

Another of Brian's responsibilities was to accompany Fred Malloy when he went hunting. Every week, Fred and the older boys would take the zebra-striped Jeep to hunt gazelle, impala, or zebra for our dinners. After they returned, we would all gather around to hear stories about their adventures.

Fred and the Zebra-Striped Jeep

Here's a story that involves that amazing zebra-striped jeep.

Fred and his Hadzabe bushman tracker were driving to Arusha for

*Brian, Jane, and Todd with
Fred's jeep*

supplies near dusk. When they passed an acacia tree, a leopard leapt off the tree, chased down the jeep, and jumped into the open vehicle, no doubt reacting to the zebra markings and the movement of the truck.

The massive cat attacked, slashing his claws across Fred's chest. Fred grabbed his rifle and slammed it into the leopard's snout. The bushman jumped out of the jeep and started running.

The leopard chased after the bushman. Within seconds, the cat was savaging the tracker, biting his arm and clawing his chest and stomach.

Fred later said he thought the bushman was going to die unless he took the shot, so he fired a round at the leopard. With his injuries and weakened condition, he missed both the cat and, fortunately, the man, but the rifle report frightened off the leopard.

Forty-five years later, Brian was at a campfire, swapping yarns with Hadza bushmen. He had just told this story of Fred, the tracker, and the leopard when, across the fire, an elderly bushman slowly rose, dropped his cloak, and revealed horrific scars disfiguring his arm and torso.

He said, "That tracker was me."

*The dining hall mural,
55 years later*

The Kiomboi Dining Hall

The dining hall was naturally one of our favorite places in the school. It was dominated by a clever mural of whimsical paintings of zebras, hippos, giraffes, and lions painted by Sissy, Fred and Martha's daughter. I was small and unsure of myself most of the time, but Fred told me all those animals were nice, and they were there to watch over little people like me.

The Malloys established a rotating seating

My desk

schedule in the dining room, which meant each of us had a chance to eat at Fred's table. Fred mostly ate pasta due to stomach problems. Because I wasn't a big fan of game meat, my favorite times were when I could sit with Fred and share his spaghetti.

When Brian and I returned to the school 55 years later, we found that little had changed. The dorms were the same. The *shamba* was still there. Even my desk stood in the exact same place. The dining hall is now a library, but Sissy Malloy's animal mural is still as fresh and beautiful as the day I first saw it. I sat in the very desk I had in first grade.

THE END OF OUR EAST AFRICAN MISSION

As a child, I was unaware of the more serious events happening during our years in Tanzania. For example, one of the students sent to the Magamba school was a Sudanese student whose parents had been assassinated, and who was himself marked for death. Although Dad was concerned that he would demand

Dad with John Garang at his graduation from Grinnell College

134

The end of the Austin

special treatment and disrupt classes, John Garang de Mabior was an excellent student and natural leader. He ultimately made Head Prefect.

After we moved back to the States, Dad sponsored John's college education, and he earned a BA in Economics in 1969 from Grinnell College in Iowa, then studied economics at the University of Dar es Salaam. After that, he returned to Sudan to lead the freedom fighter movement. He became the Vice President of Sudan and brought peace to that country for the first time in decades. This came to a tragic end in 2005 when his helicopter crashed under mysterious circumstances.

Our situation turned from adventurous to terrifying in 1964, when Tanganyika and Zanzibar united to become the Republic of Tanzania. This was after the bloody Zanzibar Revolution when it became Africa for Africans. American teachers, doctors, social workers, and headmasters were no longer welcome. It didn't affect us as much on the mainland, but it was clear that new ideas and beliefs were now in vogue.

The Kiomboi School semester was over, and we took the bus to Moshi where Mom picked us up. When we got home, Dad wasn't there and hadn't been seen for three days.

The local police brought him home two days later. The Area Commissioner had charged him with plotting to overthrow the government of Tanzania. It was no coincidence that the AC had received his training in the People's Republic of China.

A week after this happened, Dad's brakes failed when he was driving home on the steep mountain roads. Cutting a victim's brake cables was a common form of assassination in Tanzania. Dad stopped the runaway Austin by crashing into the side of the mountain. He got out and walked home.

The next week, we received our deportation papers, packed our belongings into camphor wood crates and 55-gallon oil drums, and started the process of moving back to the United States.

The Trip Home

We took our time on the journey back to the United States, stopping in several countries along the way. We visited a former headmaster of Magamba in Norfolk, England. We celebrated Easter in Sweden with Dad's Aunt Lilly, who was mushroom chef to the king of Sweden. Following that, we traveled to Venice, where I remember a nighttime gondola ride, the glassworks on the Isle of Murano, and the pigeons of San Marco landing on my head. We looped over to Denmark's Tivoli Gardens, and finally to Paris and its magical Eiffel Tower. After Europe, we left for the United States, where my first memory was visiting the New York World's Fair.

Venice gondola ride

PART FOUR

*Growing Up
and a Return to East Africa*

LIFE AFTER TANZANIA

Here's a fast-forward of 20-some years. After returning from Tanzania, I grew up in Rockford, Illinois, learned to play trumpet, went to Augustana College, met a beautiful woman, went to graduate school at De Paul University in Chicago, and married that beautiful woman.

On a side note, when I met my future wife at Augustana College trumpet auditions, neither of us knew both our sets of parents had also attended Augustana and knew each other. That may have explained why we had so much in common: music, sports, movies, and perhaps most importantly, chocolate mint ice cream.

Since Tanzania, I had not traveled beyond the Midwest state parks and forest preserves. Julie's family had, of course, done the same, visiting relatives in Michigan for every holiday. So, in true Julie fashion, she decided we should break the mold and spend our honeymoon on the gulf coast of Florida. The sand, living mollusks, and seashells in the surf were spectacular and reminded me so much of the Indian Ocean. I spent hours excitedly telling Julie my happy memories of Kigombe Beach.

After that trip, I visited my dad in Rockford to show him the shells we'd collected. He looked them over, then reached for an old Bering Biscuits tin that he kept on a shelf near his favorite chair. Inside were shells and other treasures from Kigombe. He unwrapped them slowly, one by one, handing each to me so we could admire them together and discuss exactly when and where we had found them.

I realized there was only one thing to do. "Dad," I said, "We need to go back to Tanzania. I could show Julie where we lived. We can visit the beaches and go on safari. It'll be great!"

Dad said, "We'll have to ask your mother. She's right upstairs."

We went up the stairs, sat Mom down in the living room, and presented our grand plan, to which she responded, "Absolutely not. That part of our lives is over."

Well, that was discouraging. I drove home and told Julie the entire saga. Her answer was, "If we don't make it happen, it never will."

With that, we returned to Rockford, armed with every possible argument to persuade Mom. When she opened the door to greet us, her first words were, "When are we leaving for Tanzania?"

She welcomed us into a group hug, and we started making plans that afternoon.

It was a magical year of organizing logistics and saving money for the trip. We first made a detailed itinerary and then bought consolidator airfare tickets on TWA. I signed up for several jobs at a temp agency to help pay with finances. I shuffled paperwork for a visiting nurses' company, shoveled snow at 4:30 a.m. after a blizzard, and, best of all, served Pepperidge Farm Thanksgiving cheese samples while dressed as a giant turkey with a pilgrim hat. Selfie photos weren't a thing back then and I'm devastated that I don't have a photo of me in that costume. I got the money, though.

SAFARI 1986

Our TWA flights took us to London and on to Nairobi, where our first order of business was to change money. Second, to rent a car.

We had booked rooms at Nairobi's Ambassador Hotel because we knew it was a dependable place for business travelers, with comfortable rooms and lovely common areas. However, now the entryway was a main stop for all the local buses. I have never seen so many people on one city block in my life!

The next morning, we loaded the rented sedan and headed upcountry to Hell's Gate National Park, near Lake Naivasha. We happily and confidently navigated our way with Julie's compass. We made good progress, until we passed a sign saying we were on the road to Mombasa. We were heading in the wrong direction! Pro tip: Don't use a compass designed for the northern hemisphere below the equator because it will point in the wrong direction.

Fischer's Column

Hell's Gate

Hell's Gate! Our first park that would have big game to photograph! It's a marvelous little park that has extinct volcanoes and gorges that feature two volcanic plugs. It also has lots of bird species, Cape buffalo, impala, gazelle, and zebras. But my favorite animal is the klipspringer. They are small antelope that navigate the sheerest of cliffs and boulders with pointed hooves that allow them to stand on an area the size of a dime. They communicate with their mates in sharp whistles. And, they're cute.

Hell's Gate ranger and Todd

Later in the afternoon, we reached the venerable Lake Naivasha Country Club in time for a late lunch. The spread was amazing, but when the bill came, we knew we were in trouble. The cost was 30% of the entire trip's food budget. What did we miss? The bill, of course, was in Kenyan shillings, not dollars.

A Delayed Flight

After visiting Hell's Gate, we drove back to Nairobi to catch our flight to Tanzania for our main safari. I had prebooked a four-day tour with Lion Safari, and they were to pick us up at Kilimanjaro International Airport. But after several delays, we discovered that our flight out of Kenya had been canceled.

At that point, we debated if we should wait but ultimately decided to trust the gate agent. As the delay dragged into five, then six, then seven hours, we continued to wonder whether we should have taken the overland bus through the Namanga border. By that time, however, we were stuck with our plan. After a ten-hour wait, we were put on a flight to Dar es Salaam, and we traveled from there to Kilimanjaro International.

We arrived at Kilimanjaro at 2 a.m. We stumbled over to pick up our luggage and saw, coming down the belt single file, a shirt, my shoe, some socks, a sack of camping gear, and a pair of safari pants. Someone had broken into our bags, making off with all our jeans and T-shirts, but taking none of our safari clothes. Another problem was that they neglected to tell the immigration officials we were coming from Dar instead of originating

Waiting on the airport curb

in Kenya, so there was no one at the immigration window. Someone ran to wake that guy so he could stamp our papers. Despite all this, including the unexpected hour and change of airport, a driver from Lion Safaris waited at the curbside to take us to our beloved Safari Hotel.

Arusha

Once we reached the Safari Hotel, we quickly saw nothing was the same as it had been twenty years before. The once beautiful hotel was now partly in ruins. The bar, common area, and several rooms were dilapidated. Starlings hopped in and out of broken windows.

The careworn version of the New Safari Hotel

We had not realized that Idi Amin's brief war with Tanzania had affected the entire country. In 1979, the elite Tanzania People's Defense Force drove the Ugandan army out of Tanzania and Idi Ami into exile. The army had lodged at this hotel.

At the desk, I exchanged nearly all our U.S. dollars for Tanzanian shillings. The desk clerk was more than happy to do so, handing me a towering stack of crumpled shillings.

Our driver, George, looked at that and said, "Uh-oh. You changed way too much money!"

He turned out to be right. And that was another surprise—Tanzania was bankrupt because of the war with Uganda. That stack of shillings was worthless, and no one would take anything but US dollars.

Lake Manyara

The first stop on our grand safari was Lake Manyara. It looked and felt exactly the same as when I was four years old! There was a small museum at the front gate with zoological exhibits representing all the fauna of the park. Just inside the park stood a clearing on the left. I remembered elephants grazing there—and there they were again!

Along a small stream, two impalas grazed. As we watched, one leapt

My first real live nature photo

Julie and Todd at Lake Manyara

to the other side. I thought the other would follow, so I focused on him and waited. When he did jump, my Nikon N200 fired away at a blistering three frames a second. Because this was a film camera, I had no idea if it was a good shot. When I got home and saw the picture, it showed a perfect, all-out impala leap! I printed and framed it. This was the first photograph that led me to believe I could be a good photographer.

Lunch time was pure magic! We stopped at a place called Simba Springs, a lovely spot where hippos basked in the pond. Across the water were wildebeest, zebras, and lots of birds. George unpacked boxed lunches of sandwiches and sweet Moshi bananas, and we ate right at the water's edge, just like 25 years before! To quote from the great Sam Cooke, "I haven't felt this good since I don't know when."

Ngorongoro Crater

Our next stop was the Ngorongoro Crater Lodge. Again, it was a lodge we knew from the old days. And again, it had not aged well. It's the first place I ever encountered that ran on generator power, and then for only one hour in the morning and one in the evening.

The next morning, we had a quick breakfast and waited for our required state vehicle. After several hours, we were finally told it wasn't working. When we asked about a replacement truck that *was* working, we were told there weren't any, but they could try to fix the one we'd been assigned. After another hour, they brought out the repaired state-issued Land Rover.

Everything seemed fine at first. We drove down into the Crater with no problems, but I began to feel uneasy when we saw another state vehicle just like ours, broken down on the side of the road. Two passengers stood next to it.

We called out, "Join us! It will be fun," and they piled into our car.

We saw amazing things. In 1986, the Ngorongoro Crater, like Lake Manyara, had some dirt tracks, but we could go off-road if we wanted to. So, when we spotted a lioness hunting

Our "alternate" set of brakes

wildebeest, we were able to get in perfect position to fire off some exposures (at three frames per second) as she ambushed a wildebeest. Full disclosure— continuous shooting does not mean continuous focus. The photos were pretty bad.

We noticed that our driver was passing interesting animals, and also, when he did stop, he would slowly coast instead of braking. We realized that the brakes were out, and he could only downshift to slow down.

This worked fine on the crater floor, but once the car had to travel up a steep, winding road to leave the Crater, the Land Rover's transmission gasped, wheezed, then flat-lined. There was a quiet moment when we realized we were in a car with no brakes and no transmission. Our unease shifted to concern, then to intense panic when the vehicle started rolling backwards toward a 500-foot cliff.

Our driver stopped the car by sharply turning into the side of the Crater. We waited for the engine to cool off. He was able to get the engine started, but when it died 100 feet later, the Land Rover again rolled backwards, downhill. Once more, he had to crash it into the side of the Crater to save us from plummeting off the bluff. The same thing happened three more times before we got out and started walking out of the Crater and back to the lodge.

Moshi

The next leg of our journey involved getting from Arusha to Tanga and the Indian Ocean coast. From there it would be a short, easy trip to the Usambara Mountains and our old home, Magamba. The trip was neither short nor was it easy. We had planned on an overnight train ride from Moshi to Tanga, but when George dropped us off, no one seemed to know where the train was or when it would be in Moshi again. We were passed off to George's friend,

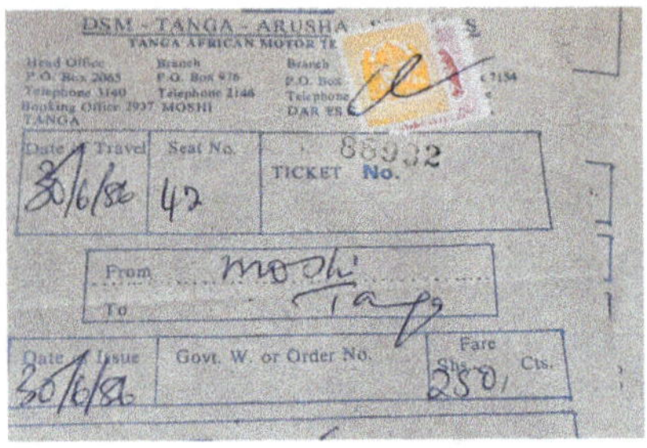

One-way ticket to paradise

the head of the Moshi post office. Although our money was useless, he was very helpful and took care of getting us four tickets on the Arusha Express Bus. He assured us it was a nonstop ride, straight to Tanga. But he also told us that if there should be a stop, we would need to get off the bus and make sure our luggage wasn't offloaded and stolen. Good safety tip!

As we waited for the bus, the postman beckoned me into a dark corner of the station, reached into his sock, and pulled out a little bag with a blue gemstone in it.

He asked, "Do you want to buy some Tanzanite? Only $50."

I said, "Sure, why not?"

He seemed a little nonplussed when I pulled out a stack of Tanzanian shillings, but he accepted them. I guess the black market isn't that choosy.

When the bus rolled up, it was like a surreal dream. It was packed with people, baskets of fruit, crates of chickens, rolled-up blankets, and mattresses. Half the windows were shattered, and the others open to the night. The postman handed us off to the bus driver for safekeeping. He examined our tickets, rubbed his face, got on the bus, and kicked four other passengers off. We got four of the six seats across the very back.

As the bus pulled out, the last words from the postman were, "Watch your luggage."

How bad could it be? Windows that don't close, luggage being stolen, and five hours crushed next to people, produce, and poultry? What we didn't know was that the trip would not be five hours, but ten.

The roads were bumpy and riddled with potholes ranging from the size of a dinner plate to as large as a car. The bus driver viewed the holes as a challenge, never changing course or slowing down to avoid them. About every twenty seconds, the bus would careen into a particularly deep one. Bags, boxes, and passengers went flying, and my head crashed into the ceiling every time.

It turned out the bus did make some stops along the way. Every ten minutes, there was someone along the road who needed a ride, so when we stopped for them, I made my way over and around the chickens, fruit baskets, and people to check on our luggage. After one of those stops, I returned to discover a new passenger had taken up residence on the seat next to me— or, more accurately, occupied both the seat next to me and my part of my seat, because she must have weighed 400 pounds. She instantly fell asleep and found a crushingly comfortable spot on my shoulder. Every time we hit a bump, I would throw my elbow into her side and use the bus's momentum to reposition her so I could breathe. I usually had 10 seconds or so before she snuggled back onto my shoulder.

At around 3:00 a.m., the bus driver announced that we would take a break in Korogwe, a town near the Usambara mountains, no bigger than a crossroads. I got off the bus to do my luggage check, then decided to investigate the roadside tavern. It was like stepping into a wild mash-up of famous films.

Picture a combination of the cantina in *Star Wars* and the Himalayan bar at the beginning of *Raiders of the Lost Ark*. It was barely lit—made dim by the hard-packed dirt walls, smoke-blackened ceilings, and meager illumination of wall torches and tabletop candles.

At one table sat a thin man wearing a desert robe, looking like an extra from *Lawrence of Arabia*. At another were two rough-looking fellows in turbans who stopped their card game to glare at me. A tall, silent Maasai warrior stood in the corner, holding a spear. I plainly did not belong there, so I discreetly left to resume my seat on the bus among my docile companions.

Tanga

We pulled into the Tanga bus station at 6 a.m. Fortunately for us, the bus driver told the taxi driver about our situation. Mr. Taxi Driver drove us to the Mkonge Hotel and spoke to the manager on our behalf.

This hotel was right on the Indian Ocean, with views of the beach from the dining room. After we settled in,

The Mkonge Hotel

we went to lunch and ordered pasta and prawns. The food seemed to be taking a long time, but we figured out the reason when we saw a fisherman hauling in a net full of prawns from the reef. Twenty minutes later, we devoured the freshest and most savory seafood we've ever eaten.

Tanga was only a step away from our old home. We just needed to find someone to drive us to Magamba and Dad's school. The hotel staff said they would make inquiries. While they were doing that, we visited many of our favorite places in Tanga, including the bookstore, toy store, Tanga Beach Club, and the Twiga Hotel with its rooftop restaurant.

After three days, we failed to find anyone who had the time, vehicle, or skill to drive up the mountain to the school. As painful and emotionally difficult as it was, we decided to forgo that part of the trip, and instead departed for Kenya via the Horo Horo border post.

We were offered a car ride up to the border, again on jouncy, bouncy, jolting roads. At the border crossing, officials charged a $3 crossing fee. We had just enough for that, and proceeded north into Kenya.

Mombasa

Once we arrived in Mombasa, the difference was immediately apparent. It seemed as if we had entered the Emerald City after enduring a yellow road made of rocks and full of potholes. Palm trees and bougainvillea brightened the curbside along a blessedly smooth tarmac road. Along the way to our resort, we passed picturesque villages and caught views of the clear, aquamarine ocean and the powdery, white sand of Diani Beach. Julie had found the Tradewinds Resort in a guidebook. It sounded like the perfect place for rest, recuperation, and recovery after our struggles in Tanzania. Just offshore lies part of the world's longest fringing reef, stretching 850 miles along the coast of East Africa.

That afternoon, we explored the beach and met the boatman. We made friends and agreed on a plan for him to take us snorkeling on the reef every day. With his guidance, we explored

Diani Beach

the reef's wonders—anemones, cowries, cone shells, octopus, and powder blue tangs. This was the principal reason we had returned to East Africa. Every day on the reef felt relaxing and fulfilling.

I reserved a day to take Mom and Dad on a Mombasa city tour. Julie remained at the hotel, saying she would stay by the pool.

Historically, Mombasa had been the launch point for expeditions and safaris. John Henry Patterson wrote the book, *The Man-Eaters of Tsavo*—a chronicle of the deadly lion attacks on railway workers in Mombasa during the 1800s. In it, he lists items needed to outfit a safari. His advice in 1907 included, "For clothing, go to Moi Avenue in Mombasa. Look up Madhavji and Sons and get measured."

That's exactly what I did. Madhavji and Sons was still there! The walls of the shop were lined floor to ceiling with bolts of cloth, every textile a different shade of khaki. They helped me choose the type and color of fabric while they measured me for a safari jacket. That afternoon, it arrived at the hotel's front desk!

And it was in Mombasa that I first witnessed Julie's organizational superpower. While we were busy in the city, she coordinated a plan with the hotel concierge to get us to Magamba. By that afternoon, we had a driver and were booked on a four-day trip back to Tanzania, expressly to visit Magamba Secondary School!

Usambara Mountains

Our driver, Joseph, had a new Toyota van that made it easy to travel anywhere. What wasn't easy was crossing the border with only Tanzanian shillings. The officials demanded American dollars, convinced that we were fat-cat Americans, flush with cash, when the truth was the opposite. We had spent the last of our dollars at the Kenya border. We were able to convince them we would soon be meeting friends in Tanzania who would give us more money. They made a note of it and allowed us across the border.

After that, we sat back and took in the scenery. Joseph drove us through Tanga and out onto the coastal plain to the base of the Usambara Mountains. Driving up the mountains and winding through the villages of Mombo, Vuga, Bumbuli, Soni, and finally Lushoto, brought to mind days gone by.

Usambara Mountains

We had chosen the Lawns Hotel as our base of operations in the Usambaras. It was one of the oldest hotels there, with a history dating back to the days of the great white hunters, when it was a lavish mountain retreat, perfect for escaping the heat of the African plains. Its guest registry included Theodore Roosevelt, Kaiser Wilhelm, and the Prince of Denmark. Unfortunately, the reality was that its days as a luxury hotel were as defunct as the great white hunters.

After checking in, we met the manager, the Welshman, who welcomed us and showed us our rooms. The room's desk was propped up with a book under one leg, and the bathtub featured faded, cracked stonework reminiscent of Roman baths. No food was available from the kitchen, and they had no clean drinking water. As challenging as this was, nothing could take away our happiness. We were finally close to Magamba Secondary School.

Dad's old classroom

Magamba Secondary School

The school looked the same, but also oh-so different. The buildings were just as they had been twenty years before. But now, used and dusty, they were in need of maintenance, or at least a new coat of paint. The old-growth forest surrounding the school was gone and replaced with small eucalyptus trees.

Dad was greeted as a returning hero when we arrived at the school. Faculty members, thrilled to see him, insisted on giving us a VIP tour. They asked him to sign the guest registry in his old headmaster's office. In his science lab classroom, he stepped up to the chalkboard and sketched zoological diagrams that would make Linnaeus proud. It was one of the best moments of the trip.

Escape From the Lawns Hotel

That night, as we packed up to go, there was a knock at the door. It was the Welshman. He wanted to know exactly how we were going to pay for our stay. I handed him a stack of Tanzanian shillings but feared the worst.

His response was, "This is a problem. Follow me."

Dad and I followed him to the back of the hotel, through a small hedge, and to a lone building with shuttered windows. Light shone out from the partially open door. The Welshman stopped on the path near the door.

He said, "The Greek will meet you in there. Explain to him how you will pay the bill."

We were ushered in by what I took to be a bodyguard and heard the door close behind us. The man they called The Greek—bald as a cue ball—sat behind an old wooden desk and looked at us as impassively as a Bond villain. The security guard stood in the shadows by the door. I could sense more than see the pistol in his belt.

He opened the conversation, saying, "I understand we have a problem. Please explain."

Dad made himself look taller and more professorial, then spoke in his no-nonsense voice. He explained why we were in Magamba, how we had changed all our US dollars for Tanzanian shillings, and why that was all we had to pay for hotels and border fees for the rest of the trip.

The Greek looked at the guard standing by the door and said, "Leave us."

When the three of us were alone, the Greek briefly glanced at me, then smiled at Dad.

He said, "Here's how it is. Your shillings are worthless, but I know who you are. I know how much you have helped Tanzania and the Magamba students. I understand your problem. If we can't help each other, why are we here?"

He reached into the desk, then handed us three $100 bills.

He said, "You will take these. You will go to the bank in Tanga, and the banker will give you smaller bills to use for other payments. I will write you a note that will make most problems go away. When you get home, you will send money in this amount to my daughter in Australia. If you do this, perfectly, no one will know I'm here."

With the Greek's money, we were able to stop at the bank in Tanga for our border crossing paperwork and for smaller bills. While Dad and I took care of that, Mom and Julie waited in the car. When we returned, there was the unmistakable aroma of samosas in the car. Samosas were a traditional treat for us—triangle pastries filled with Indian spices. Some were good and others were great, the best being from a little shop in Tanga called Patwas.

"Hey, wait a second. We're in Tanga and I smell samosas."

Mom and Julie looked sheepishly at the grease-stained paper bag, empty except for a few samosa crumbs.

"We really wanted to save some for you, but I don't know what happened," Mom blurted out.

Our driver gladly took us to Patwas and refilled the bag for Dad and me—and him.

Filled with samosas and great memories, we hopped in the van and drove back to Mombasa.

Mombasa, Again

I'll spare you the details of our trip back—crossing the border, traveling through checkpoints, negotiating bribes, engaging with drunk women with machine guns—and skip to our return to the Tradewinds Lodge. We were back in paradise, snorkeling, relaxing on the beach, and eating great food, but with no plans for our last days in Africa. We had a flight date but no plan to get to Nairobi. Again, Julie came to the rescue! She spoke to the concierge and booked a four-night camping safari through Tsavo and Amboseli National Parks.

Camping

We found that camping means different things to different people. In our case it meant a driver and a guy who purported to be a cook, an old van, two pup tents, and a couple of blankets. It didn't matter. We were up for the adventure.

We arrived at the Tsavo gate close to sundown. Our driver was not happy about going into the park that late, but we convinced him it would be fine. I'm not sure why he listened to us when we knew nothing about the campsites or even the size of the park.

Tsavo is a huge game park. We drove, and drove, and drove, and it was full darkness when we got to the camp. While the cook built a small campfire and started cooking our meals, Julie and I set up our tent by flashlight.

Nearby, we could hear giggling and crashing sounds. My parents, our campsite neighbors, were scrambling and thrashing in their collapsed tent. After we helped free them, they admitted they knew nothing about camping. The four of us together successfully raised their tent.

Afterwards, we sat down to a cooked meal around the campfire and realized two things. The first was that our cook did not know how to cook, and the second was that they only built the fire because our driver thought it would scare away wild animals.

Julie pointed toward our driver's campsite, and said, "Wait a minute. What happened to their tent?"

The drivers—our protectors—had abandoned the site and escaped to the van. As we looked their way, we heard the door locks click shut!

She then asked, "This is going to be okay, right? We're safe here, aren't we?"

We zipped ourselves into our small tent, which now seemed even smaller—some might even call it bite-size—and stayed awake listening to large predators sniffing around the campsite and the screams of small animals being killed. I had no trouble staying warm with a terrified Julie draped over me.

Camping with Julie

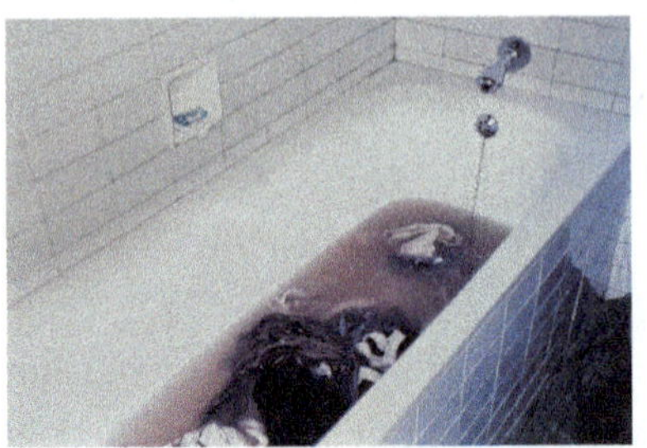

Why we don't camp

Into the Bush

We survived the night. However, we weren't too reassured after finding leopard tracks right outside our tent. Elephants walked through the campsite while we breakfasted, watched by a pride of lions about 100 meters away. Although I didn't know how we'd sleep that night, at least I knew we'd get some great photos during the day!

And we did. During our safari in Tsavo and Amboseli, we had so many opportunities—lions, elephants, Cape buffalo, even a herd of fifty giraffes. Best of all were three cheetahs jumping and playing on a dead tree. We also had stunning views of Mount Kilimanjaro and Mzima Springs. Our experiences during this part of the trip were among the most spectacular I've had in 37 years of travel through East Africa.

After one of our game drives, the driver pulled into the Amboseli Serena Lodge for lunch. We were stunned. Here was this beautiful, modern lodge right inside Amboseli National Park. It was clean, classy, and comfortable. The dining area had waiters, cold drinks, and excellent food. Plus, there were no wild animals walking through it and killing things! Were we even allowed to be there?

Julie then voiced the question we were all thinking, "Why did we decide to camp?"

When we did our laundry at our Nairobi hotel, we had more of a definitive statement than a question. *Here's why we shouldn't camp.*

REAL LIFE AFTER TANZANIA

We flew home with our camera gear, film, and a new way of viewing the world and the possibilities it offers. Julie went back to work at EDS Federal, and I finished my master's degree in trumpet performance at DePaul

The Steve Edwards Orchestra Horns: James Perkins, Steve Berry,
and Todd

University. I played with lots of great musicians and made a career for myself playing and recording big band, jazz, pop, soul, R&B, and classical music.

Julie moved up the corporate ladder. Raising a family of three children and settling into Midwest suburban life became our priority. We bought a small fixer-upper and fixed it up. Then we bought a bigger fixer-upper and really fixed it up. I printed a dozen photos from our East African adventure that hung on our walls for eleven years. One evening, as we were watching TV, Julie looked at the pictures on the wall and said, "We need to put new pictures up."

My question was, "What should we replace them with?"

Her answer? "With the new pictures you get on the next safari, when we take the kids and show them East Africa. And let's bring your mom and dad."

WOODWORKING

As a side note, I honed my carpentry skills as I fixed up the fixer-upper houses. I bought a few power tools, built a shop, and established my own woodworking company. I rebuilt houses, remodeled kitchens, made

A ten-foot-tall library

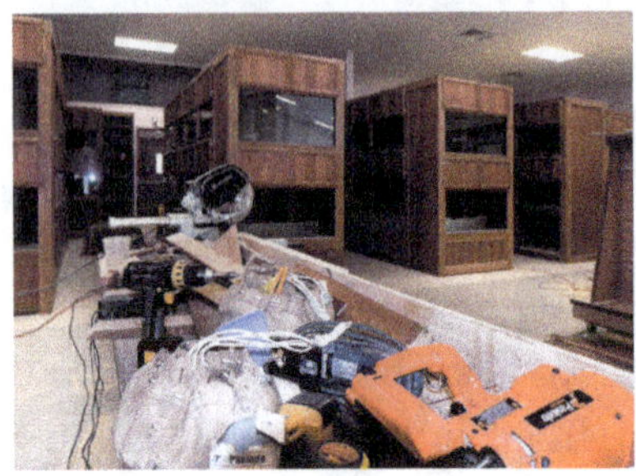

*Building Wet Pets in
Pittsburgh*

custom libraries, and designed and constructed custom furniture.

Along the way, I met Mike, who had a marvelous business called The Living Sea Aquarium. He and I became great friends, and I ended up building five expansions to his store, plus aquarium stores in Chicago, Crystal Lake, Cedar Rapids, Janesville, Indianapolis, Pittsburgh, and Orlando, among others.

An Unexpected Trip

I spent years crafting custom woodwork—often for clients who wanted aquariums that looked less like tanks and more like architectural centerpieces. One such job came through Mike, who asked me to visit the home of Aris, a legendary Chicago restaurateur and Greek tycoon. The project? Design cabinetry to house a two-sided aquarium—visible from both the kitchen and the dining room.

From a technical standpoint, it was straightforward enough. The cabinetry needed to match two very different aesthetics, one being whitewashed oak in the kitchen and the other, dark cherrywood in the dining room. The artistic challenge? I realized that each room had been styled in different Greek architectural motifs. And thanks to my favorite college course, Ancient Greek History, I saw it immediately. Doric columns in the kitchen, Ionic pillars in the dining room.

Aris loved the concept. He clapped his hands and took me on a spontaneous house tour. In his booming Greek accent, he said, "You know, Todd, we're still moving in. We need some art for the walls. Mike says you are a great photographer, eh?"

I gave a modest shrug and admitted that yes, I'd traveled the world photographing wildlife.

"Good," he said. "Talk to my wife. Maybe you can make some prints for the kids' rooms. They love animals."

Then, with a sparkle in his eye, he pointed to a massive blank wall above the fireplace. "But I need something bigger. See that space? Have you ever been to Athens?"

"Yes," I replied, "though it's been a while." I had broken my collarbone at the Acropolis when I was three.

He leaned in. "Do you have photos of the Acropolis that would fit an eight-by-twelve-foot space?"

"No," I admitted.

He spread his arms and smiled. "What are you doing in February? I have plane tickets I'm not using. How about you and Julie go to Athens for a week? Vacation. Take some pictures for my wall."

Some offers you don't turn down.

Back home, Julie and I started planning. My brother Brian and his wife Judy signed on, too. We mapped out an epic itinerary—Delphi, the field of Marathon, the Temple of Olympian Zeus, shopping in the Plaka, a side trip to the island of Rhodes, and, of course, time to photograph the Acropolis.

Some of that went according to plan. Some didn't. But those are tales for another day.

By the time we returned from Rhodes, we'd learned that the best panoramic view of the Acropolis was from Philopappos Hill. Our homebound flight left Sunday night, so Saturday afternoon was our best chance to get the shot. Our taxi dropped us off at the hill's summit with its sweeping views of Athens—and a fully scaffolded Acropolis. Every inch of the monument was wrapped in steel and tarps. Not a single stone was visible. The trip, it seemed, was a bust.

Julie, ever the optimist, joked, "You could photograph a postcard. That's probably close enough." The silence that followed was thunderous. We started packing for the next day's flight home.

But minutes later, Julie returned from settling the hotel bill. She was practically glowing. Nothing could have prepared me for the words that tumbled out of her mouth. "You won't believe this," she said. "The guy at the front desk told me they have been cleaning the Acropolis for the last week for a VIP investors tour. They are clearing the scaffolding tonight. Tomorrow, it's supposed to look better than it has in decades. I booked us a car for 8 a.m., and afterward, the National Museum!"

The next morning delivered blue skies brushed with elegant white clouds. From Philopappos Hill, the Acropolis stood out in all its restored glory, bathed in perfect light. The photos I captured that day became enormous prints, more than enough to impress a Greek tycoon.

The Acropolis in Athens

Woodworking Ties Directly to a Safari

Mike and I decided that he and his wife would join us on our next safari. Mike also managed a meat market in the Chicago stockyards. When he was told the owners planned a remodel of their sales offices, he asked me if I could do that. It would mean constructing new floors, walls, ceiling, desks, shelves, and lighting.

I said, "Sure!"

The owner gave me a completion date. Mike intervened and told the owner that he should throw in a bonus of two Nikon F5 cameras if I could hit that target date. We finished before the specified date, got the cameras, and were set for another East African safari!

FAMILY SAFARIS

I've loved all of those 25 years running photography safaris to Kenya and Tanzania. I tell my clients that the main goals are to be safe and have fun. And we always do. "Find a job you love, and you will never work a day in your life" is certainly true for me.

And when I had to decide about vacations with my family, what else would I recommend but safaris to Kenya and Tanzania!

SAFARI 1997

In preparation for this safari, I did a little research and practiced improving my photography skills. For gear, I bought the longest lens I could afford, a Sigma 150-600mm zoom. I chose Seattle Film Works slide/print film. I bought 300 rolls of it. Mom and Dad, Julie and the kids were with me this time. We packed our bags, flew to London, and on to Nairobi.

Our itinerary was much more organized than it had been in 1986, having prebooked the whole tour with United Tour Company. They were a well-respected company with offices in Philadelphia, Nairobi, and Arusha. We had fewer disaster/adventures, which left much more time and energy to enjoy the safari experience with our children, and for taking more and better photographs.

Nailed It!

The new Nikon F5 camera was amazing and our photographic chances during this trip were quite good. I hoped and prayed I had fantastic pictures, but because this was still the age of film, I really had no idea how the photos would turn out. The highlight (or low point) was going to be when we returned home and opened the box of processed negatives from Seattle Film Works.

The box arrived. I gingerly took out the top envelope and pulled out the 4 x 6 prints. The entire first roll—every single print—was exactly the same image. Every photo was of a baboon sitting in the middle of a dusty road off in the distance, taken though a muddy car window. I had no memory of seeing that or shooting any kind of picture like that. I opened the next envelope. It was the same shot there, too, as it was in the next 17 packages, over and over.

There was only one person who could help. "Julie!" I cried.

Julie looked at the pictures and said, "Huh. That explains our video, too."

She showed me a movie from our first day at Lake Manyara. While three elephants passed in front, a small voice in the background was saying, "Nailed it! Nailed it! Nailed it!"

Then, "Mommy! More film!" Then again, "Nailed it!" Then another, "Nailed it!"

We had given our six-year-old daughter, Jeni, a child's film camera for the trip. While we were enjoying the elephants, she was looking out of the back window, through the spare tire hanging on the back of the Range Rover, and photographing a baboon 100 yards away. Roll after roll after roll of my film!

Lake Baringo

Lake Baringo is an alkaline lake in Kenya's Rift Valley. It is simply teeming with birds and is home to hippos and Nile crocodiles. Magnificent Goliath herons stalk prey in the shallows. African fish eagles build large nests in the surrounding acacias. Photographing these lovely birds is easy by boat or by simply walking along the shore. It is an idyllic spot for a family vacation.

Our first goal was to film African fish eagles diving for fish. We rented two boats hoping to locate a pair of eagles. We found a tilapia fisherman paddling in his balsa wood canoe. We bought some fish and continued our search.

On this safari, Dana was fifteen, Jeni twelve, and Anders nine. Mom, Dad, and I rode in one boat while Julie and the kids took the other.

Jeni, living her best life, from the movie Titanic

This required teamwork. In the "serious photographers" boat, Dad and I were the photographers while Mom acted as support staff. Dad and I lumbered onto the boat with our bags of camera gear. I had my Nikon F5 film camera and 600mm lens. Dad also had his camera bag, but shortly realized he'd left the film and camera batteries in the room.

In the "fun" boat, Julie manned the video-cam to capture the drama of the eagle's dive. Anders was holding the audio mike to capture the *whoosh* of the dive. Dana served as support staff, and Jeni was the alluring figurehead, spreading her arms *á la* Kate Winslet in the "I'm flying!" scene from *Titanic*. Anders chose to aim the microphone at Julie rather than at the bird.

Let's jump to the action. Cue the fish toss into the water to tempt the eagles. One eagle swooped in—*whoosh!* He flew right past the boat and grabbed the fish.

The audio from this went something like this:

Fish eagle dive: Silent

Julie: "Wow! Did you hear that?" (Thanks to Anders's pointing the mic straight at Julie)

African fish eagle gliding to the lake

African fish eagle with a tilapia fish

Dad: "My camera is dead."

Anders: Giggles.

Dana: A slapping sound when she face-palmed her forehead.

Mom: Laughing.

What a team! I got great shots. We laughed and continued our boat safari to photograph more birds on the lake.

After we returned to our rooms and before dinner, Julie assembled everyone for a serious discussion about staying safe in wild places. The lodge was so close to Lake Baringo, there were hippos on the lawn outside our rooms, right between us and the main building.

Although appearing docile, hippos are the deadliest of all African animals. They forage on land at night and will attack anyone who gets between them and the water. And they can run surprisingly fast.

We kept to the paved walkway on our way to dinner, with our eyes never leaving the distant hippos. We then heard a booming, *WHOOOOAH, WHOOOOAH, WHOOOOAH* sound. Julie stopped the kids and said, "That's a hippo call. They're much closer than I thought. Be careful!"

Anders pointed upward and asked, "Do they live in trees?" There, on an open branch, was an enormous Verreaux's eagle owl. He called again, *WHOOOOAH, WHOOOOAH, WHOOOOAH*!

"Hippos in the trees," as Jeni coined it, was a good way to end our stay there.

River Crossings

The next stop on our safari was the Maasai Mara National Reserve in Kenya. At this time of year, the showpiece was the great migration. Every summer, millions of wildebeest and zebras cross the Mara River in search of new grass. Hundreds and even thousands at a time plunge into the river, crash into rocks and each other, traverse rough water, and try to outswim eighteen-foot crocodiles. It is an electrifying, life-and-death spectacle.

The herds are therefore cautious and alert at crossing points. Anything can spook them and prevent a crossing. Predators like crocodiles, unexpected noise, or a single car in their line of sight can all put a stop to a crossing. Guides know to keep away from the river's edge until the animals are committed to crossing.

On this trip, I had a panoramic film camera on loan from Panoramic Images. Each roll had only eight exposures and covered a wide angle of view, perfect for river crossings.

We were in our safari vehicle, keen for action, when our guide received news of a river crossing. It was "fairly close," meaning down the hill, across the plains, and around the bend of the river. We arrived in time to see a few zebras in the water and thousands of wildebeest on land, massing up at the river's edge. Their feet were almost in the water. They were poised to cross. I had the camera focused and ready.

In an example of perfect timing, a white Subaru sedan sped to the river's edge and squealed to a halt. Four German tourists bounded out, then yelled and pointed at the herd. Like a synchronized dance troupe, the wildebeest jerked their heads up, turned around, and galloped away from the riverbank *en masse*. In five minutes, not a single wildebeest was near the river.

All the vehicles near us left the crossing point. We were heartsick to have come so close to seeing a crossing. Our driver gave us a moment, then he also started reversing the van.

Just before our driver completed the turn, Anders pointed at the river and asked, "Who are those little guys?"

Six Thomson's gazelles were jumping on rocks on the opposite bank. They then leapt into the water to cross to our side. I thought, *May as well get a photo; it could be my only one of a crossing.*

As I pulled up the 600mm lens, the driver yelled, "He's coming! He's coming!"

"Who is coming?"

"The crocodile!"

And there he was, an enormous Nile crocodile, gliding toward the gazelles.

In the back of our van, the girls squeezed their fists and chanted, "Go Tommies, go Tommies!" like an incantation. Anders cheered for the

"The crocodile must eat, too"

crocodile, saying, "Go crocs, go!" I yelled profanities at a huge bush that was in my way.

The crocodile grabbed the gazelle and raised it into the air like a trophy, all barely visible to me. He then lowered his prey and floated into the clear. Against all odds, a second crocodile lunged out of the water and grabbed for the gazelle. They seemed to freeze in midair. I fired off shots at eight frames per second, just before all three disappeared into the river.

The girls were saddened and distressed by the gazelle kill, but our driver reminded them, "The crocodile must eat, too."

With our hearts still pounding, we continued our game drive along the river. We spotted ten elephants crossing the Mara, placidly walking past several big Nile crocodiles. Elephants simply don't care about crocs. The photos were lovely but lacked drama and storytelling.

The herd continued up the bank to the plains just as the sun broke from under storm clouds, brilliantly etching the clouds above and illuminating the mesas below. The elephant family lumbered up to a second herd waiting there on the plains. They raised their trunks and trumpeted a greeting, then passed each other with majestic strides.

I shot the panoramic camera as fast as I could. One of those photos was selected as a National Geographic Greeting Card for 2005.

National Geographic greeting card for 2005

TRAVELING WITH CHILDREN

When I travel with my family, it's easy to get swept up in the thrill of wildlife photography. But I've learned—sometimes the hard way— that everyone's experience matters. What's meaningful to me might be that perfect golden hour shot of an elephant dust cloud, but for the kids, it might be coloring on the veranda, playing under a fig tree, or delighting in an afternoon ice cream cone.

What follows are some of those moments. I only heard about some of them much later.

Ice Cream and Monkeys

Along Kenya's coast lie stretches of soft, powder-white beaches—an ideal mid-safari break for a family on the move. The beach resorts cater to everyone. For us, it was our love of the ocean and all things beach. The kids had the swimming pool, the shoreline, game rooms, hammocks, and yes, the ice cream stand. It turned out those scoops of vanilla and mango were just as memorable—if not more so—than any lion sighting I could film.

One afternoon at the coastal resort, I went off chasing colobus monkeys around the grounds. I was especially drawn to a troop with several snow-white babies. Capturing their mother-baby interactions was proving to be a

Traveling with our children: Todd, Anders, Dana, Jeni, and Julie

rewarding photographic challenge.

Meanwhile, Julie and the kids opted for a more relaxing activity—pool time. Little did they realize their day would be far from quiet.

The kids had spotted a sign pointing toward an ice cream stand on the far side of the lawn. First-day hotel guests, they followed the sign enthusiastically—groundskeepers giving friendly nods of direction. Julie, seasoned safari traveler that she is, escorted the trio and picked up cones for each of the kids, plus a well-earned dish of mint chip for herself.

Walking along the shaded path back to the pool, they were suddenly faced with a gang of vervet monkeys, with more vaulting from the trees around them. These little bandits had been casing the joint, waiting for targets.

Julie remembered how my dad handled meddlesome vervets. He would stomp the ground, step forward with confidence, and keep walking. She figured she had it under control. She turned to the kids and said, "It'll be fine. Watch this."

She stomped.

But before she could take another step, the head monkey stood tall on his hind legs, threw his arms in the air, and charged, full throttle, in a flailing, shrieking, silver blur. Julie screamed, dropped every last scoop of ice cream, gathered the kids like a lioness with cubs, and sprinted for safety. According to her, the staff *could* have helped . . . if they hadn't all been too busy howling with laughter and pointing from the sidelines.

To this day, my daughter Dana gets an eye twitch if I even *mention* monkeys in conversation. Pictures of monkeys? Absolutely off-limits.

Birds, Beaches, and Bikinis

On Kenya's north coast sits a gem of a beach resort called Hemingway's. Legend has it that Ernest Hemingway spent time there before traveling up-country to write *The Snows of Kilimanjaro*. True or not, the resort was luxurious, with white sand, a turquoise lagoon, and studded with coral islands just offshore, begging to be explored.

When we weren't out traveling the Swahili Coast, the kids made the most of the pool, which became ground zero for laughter, cannonballs, and epic splash fights. A few other families seemed to be on the same safari schedule, and our kids quickly fell in with new friends. One such companion was a chic Italian girl, whom Dana confidently declared to be rich. "She wore *five* different swimsuits yesterday."

And then there was Jemma—a five-year-old British firecracker. One morning, I was set up along the edge of the grounds, photographing golden palm weavers as they stitched their nests high in the palm trees. With my camera, big lens, tripod, Better Beamer, external battery, and cables, I looked like a birding version of RoboCop.

Golden palm weaver

Jemma appeared beside me, unfazed by me or my photographic body armor.

"Watcha photographing, guv?" she asked, hands on her hips like a junior park ranger.

"Birds," I replied.

Without a moment's hesitation, she grinned and said, "Me dad says there's only two kinds of birds—*thems with feathers, and thems in bikinis.*"

As the saying goes, you learn something new every day.

Galu Beach and Chocolate

And, speaking of monkeys.

The white-sand coastline stretches from Mombasa all the way to the Tanzanian border, growing quieter and more untouched the farther south you go. This year, we had a week-long break in our safari. Galu Beach was a serene haven of whitewashed Swahili architecture where arched verandas welcomed ocean breezes and framed views of lush tropical gardens.

After two weeks on safari, even the familiar streets of Mombasa felt exciting, a coastal wonderland to

The kids' room

*The vervet monkey in the kids'
room*

explore. At one point, after staring in a local shop window, Jeni ran up to us and squealed, "They have candy!"

We entered the chocolate store and granted permission for each child to pick out two treats. Dana chose caramel-filled chocolates, Jeni went for dark, and Anders stuck with classic milk chocolate. My parents, faithful to childhood favorites, picked Hershey bars. Julie and I filled a bag with crackers and snacks, then popped and enjoyed a tube of Pringles potato chips right on the store's steps before heading back to the bungalow.

As a clever bit of parental negotiation, we told the kids they could only have their chocolates after a nap. They dutifully trooped to their beds.

Julie and I had barely made it to the great room downstairs when blood-curdling screams pealed from their bedroom. We raced up the stairs to find my mother wielding a bedspread like a matador's cape, flapping it at a twenty-pound vervet monkey. He had already slipped by her, and in an impossibly smooth move, snatched the kids' chocolates while racing to the balcony. All three children were frozen in a huddle on the bed.

I shouted at the monkey. He turned, regarded me with utter indifference, and leapt through the balcony door, using the railing to vault into a neighboring mango tree. There he perched for ten maddening minutes, staring straight at the kids as he unwrapped their candy bars one by one, savoring each bite like a smug little confectionery pirate.

Lake Naivasha and the Rope Swing Incident

Lake Naivasha lies just northwest of Nairobi on the edge of the Great Rift Valley. The name itself is a bit of linguistic dilemma, derived from a Maasai word meaning "lake." Its colonial title, "Lake Naivasha," essentially means "Lake Lake."

Unlike the soda lakes that dominate the Rift Valley, Naivasha is relatively fresh and surprisingly deep. While it has no outlet, two rivers feed into it, and thanks to its geologic history—its basin was formed by a collapsed volcano—the lake level manages to stay remarkably stable because its water seeps through porous volcanic rock. Crescent Island is a half-submerged ridge formed from the same sunken caldera. Hippos float through the lake's reed beds, and numerous animals inhabit the island: waterbuck,

The kids and Julie on Crescent Island, 1997

giraffe, impala, zebra, Grant's gazelle, bat-eared foxes, and a dazzling variety of birds. With no predators, it's a safe, family-friendly place for a walking safari.

Whenever I plan a Kenya trip with family in tow, we start at Lake Naivasha—specifically the Naivasha Country Club. Once the go-to getaway for wealthy whites from in and around Nairobi, it's steeped in colonial lore. Our first family safari included a two-night stay there, and Crescent Island quickly became a hit. The hikes on the island were spectacular successes, allowing the children the freedom to feel a part of the habitat and to have close-up experiences with animal species we would encounter on safari.

When we weren't hiking on the island, the kids indulged in pool time, charmed the staff into doling out ice cream, and, through their explorations, discovered a forgotten playground tucked into the corner of the property.

One morning, as I was setting out for the island on a solo photo shoot—loaded with camera gear, my vest stuffed with film, and a flash unit strapped to my belt—a trio of jubilant children intercepted me mid-step.

"Come with us! You won't believe what we found! You'll love it so much!"

They marched me straight to the playground and led a proud tour of its

The kids on Crescent Island, 2005

168

*Anders showing his
perfect technique
on a rope swing*

decaying wonders. There was a rust-mottled slide. The seesaw listed dramatically at the fulcrum, and the swing chains inspired more nervous laughter than confidence. But the rope swing—that relic still looked sturdy enough.

"Look at how it works," said Anders, grabbing the rope and dangling for a moment with theatrical flair.

It was obvious he'd never tried a proper rope swing, and I understood my role. The rope looked solid, so I took a short run, grabbed hold of it mid-line, tucked it to my chest, and launched into the air like an aging Tarzan. For a glorious second, I soared parallel to the ground.

That's when the rusted ring gave way.

In a heartbeat, I transitioned from aerial grace to vertical despair, plummeting nine feet like a dropped sandbag. As I fell through the air, it occurred to me that the aging rope swing's original instruction manual probably warned against a 6'6," 230-pounder using it. The impact knocked the wind from my lungs and—according to the kids—shook the playground with such ferocity they claimed a sonic boom was heard and felt at the Country Club. One even insisted it triggered a tidal wave across Crescent Island.

I didn't know about any of that. I just knew my back somehow wasn't broken, though my eyeglasses had transformed into a figure-eight sculpture that would take days to bend back into something resembling wearable optics.

Mayan Ruins at Tikal

I was contracted to photograph Mayan ruins for a German calendar company and turned it into another chance to take my family on an adventure photo shoot. The temple complex at Tikal is a Mezzo-American religious site with at least 200 temples. Its location deep in the Guatemalan jungle qualifies it as a destination at the ends of the earth. Some of the more important temples are the Temple of the Jaguar, Temple ll, the Temple of the Masks, and Temple IV, a ruin featured in one of the Star Wars movies. The site is littered with sacrificial stones and a sprawling acropolis, and is in a constant battle with the surrounding jungle that strives to reclaim the ancient ruins.

This was the backdrop for our jungle trek. With the main acropolis plaza as our primary goal, we filled our water bottles and consulted a map. As it was our first day in this location, Julie hired a local guide who shared with us natural history and tales of the Mayan Empire. He led us unerringly through the jungle, past crumbling ruins to the Central Plaza. His morning tour complete, he advised us of which temples we could climb, the locations of other points of interest, and the best time to begin the return journey.

The Sacrificial Stone

I felt overwhelmed by the number of dramatic structures that surrounded the plaza, while Julie and the kids were intrigued by the temples and which they would climb first. As I wandered the plaza looking for the best place for a wide-angle shot of the Jaguar temple, they made a beeline for the imposing Temple ll.

My preferred way to visualize a wide-angle shot is to actually look through the viewfinder to confirm what the framing of the shot will be. The Jaguar Temple shot was complex. It would include the temple, just the right amount of surrounding jungle, some dramatic clouds, and some foreground grass. The shot looked weak. There was nothing of interest in the foreground to balance the stunning cumulus clouds over the temple. I was looking through my camera, maneuvering backwards, searching for the right foreground, when . . . Wham! As I backed up, I was "table-topped" by a three-foot-high sacrificial stone. I lay on the ground like a flipped turtle, cameras and the contents of my pockets littering the plaza. I

Temple II and sacrificial stone

got to my knees, looked around, and saw that I was alone. I dusted myself off and photographed the Jaguar Temple, but this time with a sacrificial stone in the foreground. Later, I was joined by the kids and Julie. I asked them if the temple climb was worth it.

"Oh, yeah! The views are amazing. We could see all over the place! And *you* had a spectacular fall! You hit the stone there, and didn't just go down—you tried to save yourself and spun around on one foot, put your arms out like you thought you could catch yourself, and *man*, when you went down, it was really *loud* up here."

It seemed I had added another chapter to the book, "Dad's epic falls."

Saved by Anders

Later that day, the kids found a refreshment stand that sold fresh fruit. I took the opportunity to fulfill my photo obligations. Panoramic Images had provided me with a huge 6 x 17 camera that was tailor-made for this shoot. Each frame is roughly 2 x 7 inches, with each roll containing eight exposures. I framed the shots and composed the final image by looking through an independent viewfinder mounted on the top of the camera. My first planned shot was from the top of the North Acropolis. Looking through the viewfinder, I could see the entirety of the plaza, everything from the Temple of Masks to the Jaguar Temple, with the South Acropolis in between. I made shot after shot, including more jungle on the left or right side of the frame. I was so happy with the entire situation, I loaded a second roll of film and

A 6 x 17 photo of the South Acropolis

exposed it!

When I saw Julie and the kids enter the plaza, I walked over and joined them. I must have looked pretty pleased with myself because Julie asked, "Great shoot?" Not wanting to overstate things, I replied, "Yeah. It was great." Meanwhile, a seven-year-old Anders asked, "Did you want that black thing on the lens of your camera?" I turned the camera around and stared at the lens cover in horror. It had been on the whole time! I hadn't seen it because I had been looking through the independent viewfinder. Thankfully, we had time for me to quickly reshoot the scene. This was the first of many times Anders would save me from photographic stupidity in my career.

Back at the lodge, we photographed a flock of eight ocellated turkeys before lunch and a nap.

A Hike to Temple IV

In the afternoon, we hiked back to the ruins with the rest of the day dedicated to hiking to Temple IV. When it was featured in the *Star Wars* movie, a Rebel soldier with binoculars stood atop an ancient pyramid, guiding a fighter pilot to the jungle planet's hidden base. Our route took us to the temple and led us down winding jungle paths, under the green canopies, past a ruin called the "Bat Temple," more winding paths, and finally to Temple IV. The tallest structure in Tikal, Temple IV rises 213 feet above the jungle floor. At that time, visitors were allowed to climb the original stone stairs, and it was a popular vantage point for viewing sunsets. The climb was exhilarating, and the views breathtaking. The three children had packed a picnic basket with sodas, crackers, and some fresh fruit. It was so sweet to watch them spread the feast on the stone floor at the pyramid's top as the sun set over the jungle.

I'm not sure if it was me or Julie who first thought, *Uh-oh, we need to get down from here and find our way through the jungle to our lodge—and the sun has already set! What were*

The Bat Temple

The jungle trail

we thinking? There was still some afterglow to illuminate the descent, but the jungle looked dark. Anders confirmed that we were headed in the right direction by pointing out the Bat Temple. There was still the hint of a path when Jeni ran ahead and pointed to a sign. Using what remained of our fading flashlight batteries, she illuminated a sign that had a big red circle with a line through it, covering a stick drawing of a photographer falling backwards over a sacrificial stone. Oh, how they laughed!

Now that the flashlight batteries were completely depleted—and who goes into a jungle at night with fully charged batteries, anyway—we continued along the dimly lighted path. We heard a rustling behind us that was, to me, evidence of an impending puma attack. Never mind. It turned out to be a roving squad of white-nosed coatis looking for dinner. Ten minutes later, the rustling sounded different—louder and closer. I was certain this was it. It's common knowledge that pumas lurked everywhere in the dark woods! This time, it was a group of eight ocellated turkeys. *Hang on! Wasn't there a flock of eight turkeys right by our lodge?* As soon as the thought entered my mind, we followed a turn in the path, and there was our lodge, all lit up for the evening!

You know the old saying: *All's well that doesn't end with a puma attack.*

Ocellated turkey

THE WORST DAY EVER!

I did get shots I liked on our 1997 family safari. Some were fine, some were amazing. A gallery in the Chicago area wanted to do an exhibition of the best ones. I was thrilled! I sent my 50 best negatives back to Seattle Film Works to have 20×30-inch prints made for the showing.

It took a long time for the prints to arrive, and when they did, it was a disaster! They came in a brown paper package that was torn, crumpled, and held together with adhesive tape. The prints were damaged beyond repair, and all the negatives were gone. I couldn't believe it. I told Julie I would never take another photograph in my life.

Julie, as usual, remained cool and steady. She said, "You just need to go back and take even better pictures."

THE BEST DAY EVER!

All my camera gear needed professional cleaning after that dusty 1997 safari. While waiting in line at the repair shop, a man came over and looked in my camera bag.

He said, "Looks like you have a lot of Sigma lenses there."

Rather than say, *That's all I can afford*, I went with, "Boy, they sure are great!" I didn't know it at the time, but he was the Sigma lens rep for the Midwest.

He asked if I had any prints of photos taken with the Sigma lenses. I had several 8 × 10 shots from the last safari in the car, which I showed him. He said he loved them all and called his company in New York. Right there, I signed on to become a Sigma Pro.

Later in the week, they asked if I could go to Florida to photograph egrets, alligators, and blackwater swamps for their Japanese website.

I enthusiastically agreed, saying, "Oh, yeah, I know Florida like the back of my hand."

I had only been there twice before—once for my honeymoon and once to visit Disney World.

I immediately phoned friends for advice and discovered there was a famous bird photographer in Florida. I called him and explained my project. He told me to just go to any swamp in Florida—and good luck. He was about to hang up, but then, perhaps showing mercy, asked what I liked to photograph.

I said, "East Africa. I love photographing on safari!"

He shouted, "East Africa? That's where I'm going."

"Who are you going with?" I asked.

"I don't know."

When are you going?" I asked.

"In October!" he replied

With Julie's words echoing in my head that I needed to go back and take better pictures, I cried, "That's when I'm going, too!"

He proposed a swap—I'd show him the best places to photograph birds in East Africa, and he'd teach me everything he knew about photography. We made plans for the October safari, then discussed bird sanctuaries in Florida.

For the October trip, Julie said it was time for a "big boy lens," like they use at NFL games. She was so right. My next purchase was the Nikon 600mm f/4, a *T.rex* of a lens. This was going to be serious photography.

During that October safari, I learned valuable new information and received reinforcement of skills I had before the trip. We discussed compositional framing, head angle, main subject and background, and the quality and direction of light. With these fundamentals, I sharpened my photographic vision, style, and craft.

PART FIVE

Gustafson Photo Safari

A Whole New World

I took several thousand pictures on the 1997 safari. My heart lurched and froze when I opened the big cardboard box, pulled out the first box of slides, and looked at the first picture. I had never seen anything like it from my camera.

The photo showed a yellow-billed stork fishing in a dark lagoon. He was balancing with one leg out of the water, the pink of his leg vibrant against the black pond and green water lilies. Feathers and scales popped from the

My first look at the box of slides

photo. Water drops sparkled in sharp relief on his raised leg.

I could barely grip the slides. Birds, lions, leopards, cheetahs, giraffes, waterbucks, and rhinos—stunning portraits and action shots, one after another. I sorted through them to decide which to keep and which were redundant or substandard. If any of the critical elements were wrong, such as head angle, exposure, or lighting, off it went to the discard pile. And when an outstanding photograph appeared, I was euphoric. I had never taken so many great shots in my life!

Julie on safari

My Fortieth Birthday

I had returned from that October safari in time for my fortieth birthday. Just as the party was winding down, Julie brought out a bulky gift topped with a bow. I unwrapped it and discovered I was the proud owner of a 30-gallon trash can. The card read, "For all the slides you are going to throw away."

Okay. Thanks?

She then handed me a second gift, a giant silver screen for projecting slides. The card for this one read, "For all the slides you are going to keep!"

That's my Julie.

The Mentor

In the early 1990s, during my woodworking days, I met the man who would become my best friend and mentor. He was a high-end photographer whose work had been featured in *Time, Life, Look,* and *National Geographic,* plus he was the photographer for Georg Solti and the Chicago Symphony Orchestra.

I first met Robert Lightfoot III when he needed three custom-made displays for our local library. He commissioned me to build and install these from his designs. I worked closely with him on the project and told him about photographing wildlife in East Africa. He asked to see some of my work.

Over the years, we spent long hours discussing photography. He generously critiqued my work, but was always frank about what was wrong, and likewise, was always specific about how I could improve.

The first shots I showed him, all those years ago, were of some birds. He said, "The light is a little flat."

Later, I showed him more bird photos, this time taken with my upgraded camera system. He said, "You almost captured the moment."

When I had a great shot I knew he would love, he took a long look, and said, "You need a different printer."

The Smithsonian Exhibit

Now it was the week after my fortieth birthday, and I had stacks of safari images from October, sorted into categories of good, better, and best. I called my mentor for help.

He quietly examined the first ten of my best slides, then went into the kitchen to telephone one of his friends who worked as a photo editor. They arranged for us to meet the next day in her downtown office.

At the meeting, I talked about my safari experiences while she looked at the slides. She picked up the phone and called the owner of the stock agency, who joined our meeting.

After he looked at the slides, he said, "We have a project with the Smithsonian Museum to provide images for their new permanent exhibit called *African Voices*. Can we send them your photos?"

The Smithsonian chose a dozen photos for their permanent exhibit.

A Visit to Washington, DC

Five years later, I went to Washington, DC to photograph the monuments. While there, I took a break from photography and ducked into the Smithsonian National Museum of Natural History. I walked through the entrance, down to the first floor, and around the *Asian Art Exhibit*—and there it was—*African Voices*, the exhibit of East African tribal artifacts and natural history.

After hefting cameras and lenses all day and needing a rest, I sank onto a bench to relax as I watched my images play across the 24-foot panoramic

The permanent exhibition at the Smithsonian Natural History Museum

screen. Five minutes later, a big school group came into the room.

Sixty third graders assembled in a semicircle facing the screen, gazing at the photos in awe, sometimes pointing, sometimes whispering little "wows!" and "cools!" One of the teachers sat down next to me. She looked at my overstuffed photo vest and the pile of cameras in my lap, and said, "I bet you wish you had taken those beautiful pictures."

You wait your whole life for a moment like this. I smiled and said, "Ma'am, I did take those photos."

After that, I was mobbed by third graders, asked thousands of questions about the animals in the photos and signed everyone's Smithsonian guidebooks.

St. Louis Children's Hospital

The week after the Smithsonian meeting, the Panoramic Images photo editor requested a meeting on Tuesday morning. She told me to bring my best photos of birds and animals.

At the meeting, I was introduced to a man who was designing artwork for the intensive care unit of St. Louis Children's Hospital. Four triage units would be configured to look like vintage railway cars traveling through the African savannah. Surrounding the cars would be life-sized zebras, gazelles, giraffes, and elephants, with clouds of birds in the sky.

He already had a portfolio of slide sheets on his desk. While he and I discussed my experiences in Tanzania, the photo editor gave him my stack. The buyer spent the rest of the meeting examining my slides with a magnifying glass, presumably to see if there was enough sharpness and detail for life-sized images.

After five minutes, he pushed the other portfolio to the edge of his desk and began selecting individual slides from mine. I was dumbfounded when the editor told me the rejected stack was from an acclaimed nature photographer.

This started my three-year photo project with the St. Louis Children's Hospital.

Lincoln Park Zoo

My mentor then called to tell me that designers working for the Lincoln Park Zoo wanted to meet with me. They were planning a new exhibit called *Regenstein African Journey* that would feature photographs of African animals—they would need many, basically from aardvark to zebra. They checked out my photos and I looked at their list. I could already supply 75% of what they needed.

"Don't worry about the rest," they said. "We have three years before the project will be finished."

Wow! If this wasn't the best reason to keep going back to East Africa!

People from all over the world were requesting that I take them on safari. Julie agreed it was time to create a company for tours and photography instruction. In 1999, I launched Gustafson Photo Safari to escort photographers and adventurous tourists to Tanzania and Kenya. On these trips, while I was showing clients the wildlife of East Africa and discussing photography techniques, I also kept the zoo's checklist in mind.

One of their requests was for a photo of an Abdim's stork, which is a small, black stork with red and blue facial skin. I had never seen one before, but on my first January safari with clients, I had my chance in the Ngorongoro Crater. One was perched on a rock by the side of the road.

"Stop the car NOW!" I called to the driver. "It's an Abdim's stork!"

I shot three rolls of film photographing that bird. When I was satisfied that I had the subject covered, I looked up from the camera and saw, all the way to the horizon, tens of thousands of Abdim's storks. Luckily, I still had more film.

On this trip, our group had opportunities for stunning wildlife photography. I photographed aardvark, giraffes, elephants, impalas, zebras, and wild dogs, in addition to an African farmer, marabou storks at sunset, and habitats destroyed by deforestation. All of these would be used in the

Lincoln Park Zoo project.

By the time I was done, I had managed to photograph all the animals on their checklist except different species of African cichlids. Cichlids inhabit the Great Rift Valley lakes—Lake Malawi, Lake Victoria, and Lake Tanganyika. Lake Malawi alone contains more than 500 species. However, we were nowhere near those lakes, and I had no underwater photography equipment. When I was back in the United States, I called my friend Mike at The Living Sea Aquarium. He had fifty kinds of cichlids in his store. Instead of traveling all the way to Africa, I simply drove there to photograph these odd and beautiful fish.

Lincoln Park Zoo's *Regenstein African Journey* opened in 2003 to great acclaim. They displayed my photos front and center, and they graced beautifully designed signage. My favorite is the accordion display of 8×2-foot images of animal eyes that greets visitors at the entrance.

More than 20 years later, my granddaughters enjoy visiting the zoo and seeing these exhibits.

Granddaughter Coraline at the entry to Lincoln Park Zoo's African Journey

After countless adventures and a library of breathtaking images, the moment arrived—I had the experience, the passion, and a collection of East African photographs that could speak for themselves. It was time to take that understanding and turn it outward, to share it with others. That's when Gustafson Photo Safari was formed—a company rooted in storytelling, conservation, and the thrill of seeing the wild through a photographer's lens.

PART SIX

Magamba Secondary School Becomes a University:
A Journey of Legacy, Loss, and Unbreakable Resolve

In 2008, our family received news that Magamba Secondary School would be elevated to university status. A dedication ceremony was scheduled for September, and we were all invited. First, though, I had back-to-back safaris to lead in August—two weeks of wildlife photography followed by two more filming for a television project called "The Decisive Moment." It was my first time in front of the camera, and those weeks were physically exhausting and mentally consuming.

Whenever I return from a trip, calling Mom and Dad is instinctive. I usually share the highlights and reassure them that all went well. I reached for the phone, then hesitated. I was tired. I told myself I'd call that evening.

Instead, the phone rang in my hand.

The Accident

It was my brother Brian. I'll never forget the chilling urgency in his voice when he said, "Mom and Dad were in an accident. They were on the way home from church, stopped for a car crossing the road, but the truck behind them didn't stop. It just drove right over them."

I jumped in the car and raced 70 miles to Swedish American Hospital in Rockford, where Dad had been taken. Mom had been transported to a different facility. Neither one knew where the other was. Both were in critical condition.

Dad had broken ribs, a punctured lung, and a bruised heart. Mom's injuries were different. Her knees were crushed, and her wrist was shattered. We shuttled between hospitals as medical teams addressed each trauma. While Dad's condition improved slowly, Mom's prognosis was grim. She'd likely never walk again. Her hand? A painful question mark.

During one of my visits, Dad looked at me and asked, "Do you still have those KLM tickets to Tanzania?"

"I haven't canceled them," I said, a bit surprised. "Brian and I have been, well, busy."

"Good," he replied. "I think I can go to the school dedication."

I blinked. "Did your doctor sign off on this?"

He shrugged. "He said I could die here or die in Tanzania. I might as well try."

And that was Dad—no dramatics, just quiet determination. For the next eleven days, Brian and I prepared to travel with an invalid, certain we were courting disaster.

The Return to Tanzania

As the departure date neared, Dad grew stronger, but international travel was no easy endeavor. The journey included two eight-hour flights, a transfer in Amsterdam, a 45-step descent to the tarmac in Kilimanjaro, an overnight stop in Arusha, a nine-hour drive across the country, and a mountain drive, 7,000 feet up the Usambaras, to Lushoto.

At last, we arrived at the Tumaini Hostel in Lushoto. Dad slumped in a lobby chair, drained. Then the door opened, and a man in a gold-trimmed dashiki entered.

Dad greeting a former student

His eyes scanned the room and locked onto Dad. He crossed the room quickly, fell to his knees, and said, "My headmaster!"

Dad straightened himself, lighting up with recognition. "Simon Mbishwa, my first Head Prefect."

In an instant, Dad's weariness disappeared, and he became animated, alert, and vibrant. Simon was now the bishop of the Tanga region. Life had treated him well. Then more of Dad's former students trickled into the lobby—teachers, lawyers, clergy, doctors—all thriving and shaping Tanzanian society. Brian and I went to sleep that night knowing this trip was already more remarkable and meaningful than we had imagined.

Revisiting the Past

The following morning, we toured the Usambaras. Our first stop was the old Magamba Secondary School campus. The new university had taken over the old school complex, yet echoes of Dad's influence lingered. The dining hall he designed now housed the national brass band rehearsals for the dedication ceremony.

We visited the old headmaster's office, then our former home—a tin-roofed garage structure now listing to the left but still with a familiar look. The family who lived there welcomed us inside. Their patriarch had been the carpenter who built the school's furniture when Dad was in charge. His wife entered with tea and biscuits. She told us that when Mom and Dad first arrived in 1962, Mom had invited the villagers over for high tea—a gesture she cherished to this day. She was proud to serve us in return.

Dad, the current resident, Salvatory, and Brian at the old headmaster's house

The Dedication Ceremony

By dawn, saws and hammers echoed through the valley as workers

The Maasai delegation

assembled the stage, seats, and a podium. We spent the morning with dear friends—Michael and Sylvia Chesterman—and later, the former First Lady of Tanzania, Anna Mkapa. Dad improved with each conversation, invigorated by the memories and the torrent of goodwill.

Delegations poured in from across Tanzania. The mountainsides overflowed with attendees. Maasai and Usamba Tribal people mingled with clergy and dignitaries. Hymns filled the air as Dad used his cane to climb to the VIP section, seated among university presidents and archbishops.

Michael Chesterman approached the podium. "I am the first headmaster of Magamba Secondary School," his voice rang out. He continued, "And I stand here before you for one who cannot stand—Bwana Paul Gustafson."

Thunderous applause erupted across the valley. The University of Dar Es Salaam's president and the Archbishop of Sweden lifted Dad from his seat. The crowd roared. Tribal chants rang out. Standing off to the side, I took it all in, tears of joy flooding my face and intense pride filling my heart.

Silence fell as former Prime Minister Edward Lowassa, speaking in formal Swahili, outlined the university's vision. Suddenly, six black SUVs rolled in and security flanked the stage. The president of Tanzania, Jakaya Kikwete, had arrived. He sat, listened, watched, and after the last speech had been made and the last hymn had been sung, departed silently, like a coda to the grand performance.

All of it—every improbable twist, every unforgettable moment—really happened. And it all began because one man, in the quiet basement of a Lutheran church, simply said, "Yes."

Dad being recognized at the dedication ceremony

Thanks to my Dad, Paul Gustafson
Without his courage,
none of this would have happened

ACKNOWLEDGMENTS

Life is defined by our individual viewpoint, which in turn is shaped by life experiences and the influence of those within our sphere of existence—both those we hold dear and those who may oppose us. I've learned from my parents, my siblings, my wife, and my children:

From Dad: "Tell the truth and be kind."

"There's more to life than you see in the moment."

"Leave the world a better place than how you found it."

From Mom: "Always start with dessert. You don't know what could happen."

And, her definition of nuts in bakery is "Nuts are taking the space where chocolate should be."

From my brother Brian: "If there are no elephants, lions, or giraffes around, you can always find birds to photograph."

From my middle daughter Jeni: When someone mentioned a glass that was half full or half empty, depending on your point of view, she perceptively said, "All the glasses are full. There's the liquid and there's air." And at a family gathering when discussing thinking outside of the box, seven-year-old Jeni asked, "Why does it have to be a box?"

From my son Anders when asked by a Swedish cousin if he is going to follow in my footsteps: "Those would be really big footsteps to walk in. I don't have shoes that big. I'll find my own way." He was twelve years old at the time.

From my eldest, Dana: "Avoid monkeys whatever the cost. They are devious, crafty, unreliable, and always up to something." And from an eighth grade Dana, "Plan for the future."

Last, but not least—wisdom from Julie: Photoshop and digital imaging had just become the standard for photographers. I told her, "I can take a distracting stick out of the picture. I could even add a bird or animal to the scene!" Her response has been my guiding light to this day. She said, "Can't you just take a better picture?"

I listen to people talk about events in their lives. Some view negative events as tragedies directed specifically at them by God, fate, or predestination. I prefer to view these events as part of life, for learning and change.

Memories and stories are like shiny objects to be gathered and shared. The best ones contain a lesson or point that makes the tale significant or informative. I meet many diverse, interesting people in my travels, many becoming lifelong friends. I then take the experiences—the adventures, the humorous, and even the awful—and file them away to share in the future, with some ultimately finding a place in this collection.

My thanks to Charlie Levin, my publisher, and the staff at Munn Street Press. Thanks to Don Hurzeler for suggesting I "put these stories to paper" and share them. All my love to my wife Julie for allowing me to travel the world gathering these stories. I couldn't have done any of this without my children. I am ever grateful to you Dana, Jeni, and Anders for supporting me when I'm away and for traveling with me when you can. You inspire me every day. Bless you Mom and Dad for having the courage to accept a mission in Tanganyika in an effort to make the world a better place. Thanks to you, my brother Brian, for a lifetime of love, inspiration, mentoring, friendship, and for your unique view of how things work. Thank you, Jane Goodall, for your support and friendship. Thanks to Carl Safina for your hospitality and for lending your voice-over talents to *The Natural World* documentary. I wouldn't be where I am today without the continual push to improve my photography provided by Robert Lightfoot lll. Many thanks to Doug Segal, Laurie Schoultercarol, Michelle Novak, Evan Bower at Panoramic Images, who championed my photographic work for decades. Thanks to Mike Sergey, who taught me what an f-stop is. I couldn't have photographed events in the natural world without the indispensable ground operators and driver guides: Salvatory Mremea, James Chitete, Nicholas Otaro, Euticus Maragi, Alison Mello, Yehudi Hernandez, Dirk Theron, Franco, Harendra Singh, Amit Sankala, Sanjay Pandit, Pelin Karaca, Andrea Holbrook, Charlie Munn, and Solofo. The musical soundtracks for the Ends of the Earth documentaries would not exist without Jo Ann Daugherty and Ryan Bennett. I salute Gary Fry's musical genius that brought my documentary soundtracks to life. Finally, my never-ending gratitude to Dr. Karen Hunt for her keen eye and tireless editing, for bringing the stories into focus, giving them direction, and correcting all the stuff I managed to get wrong. Whatever errors remain, I claim as my own.

PHOTOGRAPHY CREDITS

All photos were taken by Todd Gustafson with the exception of those listed below.

Cover photo by Lynda Goff
Todd and a young male cheetah in the Central Serengeti, 2024. Cheetahs climb termite hills for a high vantage point to spot prey. With no available hills in the area, this cheetah chose to get a better view from the top of the vehicle.

Photo by Yannis Arvanitis
- Page 4 Book collector John Dupps receiving his Museum Edition of the To the Ends of the Earth three-volume set

Photo by Anders Gustafson
- Page 8 The Nashville Music Scoring Orchestra

Photos by Judy Gustafson
- Page 132 The dining hall mural, 55 years later
- Page 133 My desk

Photos by Julie Gustafson
- Page 7 Todd and Gary Fry at Ocean Way Studio
- Page 139 Hell's Gate ranger and Todd
- Page 140 Waiting at the airport curb (self-timer)
- Page 146 Diani Beach
- Page 165 The kids' room
- Page 166 The vervet monkey in the kids' room
- Page 168 Anders showing his perfect technique on a rope swing
- Page 180 Granddaughter Coraline at the entry to the Lincoln Park

Zoo's African Journey
- Page 187 Todd and Paul Gustafson

Photos by Louise Gustafson
- Page 128 All four photos of Dad and an expert mechanic with our trusty Austin in various states of disrepair
- Page 131 Halloween at Kiomboi
- Page 132 Brian, Jane, and Todd with Fred's Jeep
- Page 133 Dad with John Garang at his graduation from Grinnell College
- Page 142 Julie and Todd at Lake Manyara
- Page 143 Our "alternate" set of breaks

Photos by Paul Gustafson
- Page 121 Our DC3 plane
- Page 121 Jane, Mom, Brian, and Todd having one of Mom's famous picnics on the road
- Page 122 The Safari Hotel
- Page 123 Mom in front of Flint Cottage
- Page 123 The headmaster's house
- Page 124 Jane, Todd, Mom, and our new puppy
- Page 125 One of Jane's goats and Richardi
- Page 124 Magamba Secondary School
- Page 126 Class photo of Magamba students
- Page 126 One of Mom's piano students
- Page 126 Todd, Jane, and Laurie Lindell in Tanga
- Page 127 Family and friends on Kigombe Beach
- Page 127 Brian, Jane, and Todd on Kigombe beach
- Page 134 The end of the Austin
- Page 163 Traveling with our children: Todd, Anders, Dana, Jeni, and Julie

Photo By Karen Hunt
- Page 109 Reef mantas and a trumpet player

Photo by Susana Name

- Page 10 Todd with Jane Goodall reviewing the museum edition of the *East Africa* book

Photo by Carl Page

- Page 74 A tundra-ready photographer

Photo by Cindy Soderholm

- Page 20 Shipwreck on the Mozambique Channel

Photo by Craig Williams

- Page 153 The Steve Edwards Orchestra Horns: James Perkins, Steve Berry, and Todd

ABOUT THE AUTHOR

Award-winning photographer Todd Gustafson has been filming wildlife, vulnerable habitats, and natural history around the world for the last three decades. He is the founder and tour leader of Gustafson Photo Safari, a company that escorts clients to the ends of the earth to see, experience and photograph nature's beauty. His works include the three-volume *To the Ends of the Earth* book set, *East Africa, Birds of East Africa,* and *The Natural World,* praised as the most lavishly beautiful books since *Audubon Portfolios.* When Pope Francis viewed them, he said, "With these books you have the power to change hearts and minds and make this a better world." Todd's book, *The Photographers' Guide to the Safari Experience* is a great resource for safaris to East Africa. His photos are included in each volume of the ten-book series, *Remembering Wildlife.* His *To the Ends of the Earth* documentaries, *East Africa, Birds of East Africa, The Natural World, Oceans,* and *Avian Chronicles* have aired in 36 countries and on 129 public television stations in America. Born in Moline, Illinois but raised in Tanzania, he calls both the United States and East Africa his home. He now lives in the Chicago area with his wife Julie and beloved beagle Augie. For more information, visit his website at https://totheendsoftheearthnfp.org/